Wrightslaw

Special Education Legal Developments and Cases 2016

Peter W. D. Wright, Esq.

Pamela Darr Wright, MA, MSW

Harbor House Law Press, Inc.

Hartfield, Virginia 23071

Wrightslaw: Special Education Legal Developments and Cases 2016

By Peter W. D. Wright and Pamela Darr Wright

Library of Congress Cataloging-in-Publication Data

Wright, Peter W. D. and Pamela Darr Wright

Wrightslaw: Special Education Legal Developments and Cases 2016

p. cm.

ISBN 13: 978-1-892320-40-7

ISBN 10: 1-892320-40-1

1. Law — Special Education — United States. 2. Children with disabilities — Education — United States. 3. Special education — Parent Participation — United States. I. Title.

10 9 8 7 6 5 4 3 2 1

Printing History

Harbor House Law Press, Inc. issues new editions to keep our publications current. New editions include major revisions of text and/or changes. New printings include minor changes and corrections.

First Edition September 2017

Disclaimer

The purpose of this book is to educate and inform. Although efforts have been made to ensure that the publication is accurate, there may be mistakes, typographical and in content. If you are dissatisfied with the book, please return it to the publisher for a full refund.

When You Use a Self-Help Law Book

Law is always changing. The information contained in this book may or may not reflect current legal developments. For legal advice, you should consult with an attorney.

Bulk Purchases

Harbor House Law Press books are available at a discount for bulk purchases, academic sales or textbook adoptions. For information, contact Harbor House Law Press, P. O. Box 480, Hartfield, VA 23071. Please provide the title of the book, ISBN number, quantity, how the book will be used, and date needed.

Toll Free Phone Orders: (877) LAW IDEA or (877) 529-4332.

Toll Free Fax Orders: (800) 863-5348

Contents

Introduction

If you are the parent of a child with a disability, you represent your child's interests. To effectively advocate for your child, you need to know about recent legal developments and decisions that may affect your child's educational program.

If you work as a teacher, related service provider, or administrator, you need to know about new developments in special education law.

If you are an attorney or advocate who assists children with disabilities and their families, you have a responsibility to be current on cases and other legal issues.

We wrote ***Wrightslaw: Special Education Legal Developments and Cases 2016*** to make it easier for you to stay up-to-date on new cases and legal developments.

Why You Need This Book

You need ***Wrightslaw: Special Education Legal Developments and Cases 2016*** because you want to know — or you need to know — about exciting new developments in special education law and advocacy. Exciting? Yes!

It's exciting when the Supreme Court of the United States (SCOTUS) agrees to decide two special education cases in one term, especially since the last case they decided was *Forest Grove v. T. A.*, 129 S. Ct. 2484 (2009).[1]

Special Education News in 2016

Supreme Court Grants Certiorari in Two Cases

In 2016, the Supreme Court of the United States (SCOTUS) granted certiorari in two cases: *Fry v. Napoleon* (6th Circuit) and *Endrew F. v. Douglas School District RE-1* (10th Circuit).

The primary legal issue in *Fry v. Napoleon* was exhaustion of administrative remedies. The IDEA requires that parties request a due process hearing before filing suit in Court.

In 2015, cases brought under Section 504/ADA - not IDEA - were dismissed in the 3rd, 6th, 9th, 10th, and 11th Circuits. In some of the cases dismissed, the children had never been found eligible for special education under IDEA or the relief they sought was not available under the IDEA.[2]

The primary legal issue in *Endrew F.* was the role of progress in a free appropriate public education. The Court first addressed this issue in *Hendrick Hudson District Bd. of Ed. v. Amy Rowley, 458 U.S. 176* (1982).[3]

In early 2017, the Supreme Court issued unanimous decisions in *Fry* and *Endrew F.* These cases are discussed in depth in Chapter 3.

---

[1] http://www.wrightslaw.com/law/caselaw/ussupct.forest.grove.ta.pdf

[2] *Wrightslaw: Special Education Legal Developments and Cases 2015,* pages 21-25.

[3] http://www.wrightslaw.com/law/caselaw/ussupct.rowley.htm

Cases of the Year for 2016

Wrightslaw selected four exemplary cases as **2016 Cases of the Year**:

- *AG v. Paradise Valley Unified School District*, 815 F.3d 1195 (9th Cir. 2016)
- *Timothy O. v. Paso Robles Unified School District*, 822 F.3d 1105 (9th Cir. 2016)
- *LO v. NYC DOE*, 822 F.3d 95 (2nd Cir. 2016)
- *Cobb County Sch. Dist. v. DB* (11th Cir. 2016)

In Chapter 3, you will learn what makes these four cases unique and earned them the distinction as **2016 Cases of the Year**. These cases are "must reads" for special education attorneys, advocates, and others who are interested in special education law.

Key Decisions from the Courts of Appeals

Chapter 3 includes all key decisions in special education cases from the Courts of Appeals with a Table of Decisions that makes it easier to find relevant information.

Department of Justice Initiates Discrimination Cases

In 2016, the Department of Justice initiated and settled several cases about discrimination by YMCAs, a summer camp and a Montessori school.

The DOJ initiated a lawsuit against Georgia, *U. S. v. Georgia (GNETS)*, alleging that the state has discriminated against thousands of public school students with behavior-related disabilities by segregating them in separate unequal educational programs for years.

You will find information about these and other discrimination cases initiated and settled by the Department of Justice in Chapter 2.

Policy and Guidance from ED, OSERS, OSEP, and OCR

The Department of Education (ED), the Office of Special Education and Rehabilitative Services (OSERS), the Office of Special Education Programs (OSEP), and the Office for Civil Rights (OCR) issued "Dear Colleague" letters and policy guidance in several areas in 2016:

- Students with ADHD and Section 504
- Providing Behavioral Support in IEPs
- Discrimination Against Students with Disabilities
- Civil Rights of Students with Disabilities
- Restraint and Seclusion
- Rights of Students with Disabilities in Public Charter Schools Under Section 504 & IDEA

Wrightslaw: Special Education Legal Developments and Cases 2016 includes all Policy letters and Memos issued by the Office of Special Education and Rehabilitation Services (OSERS) and the Office of Special Education Programs (OSEP) in 2016.[4]

These documents are useful when you want to know how the law is being interpreted by the Department of Education and the Office for Civil Rights, and when you need to educate school staff and administrators about their legal responsibilities.

[4] OSEP Memos about grant applications, State Performance Plans (SPP) and Annual Performance Reports (APR) are not included in this book.

If you advocate for children with disabilities, you need answers to these questions. For example:

When a parent is recording an IEP meeting, can school staff stop the recording because they believe the parent had an adequate opportunity to understand the meeting? (See OSEP Letter to Savit, p. 32)

Do parents have a right to open their due process hearing to selected individuals without opening the hearing to the public? Does the school have a legal right to object to the parent's decision to open their due process hearing to the public? (See OSEP Letter to Michael Eig, p. 35)

After a school evaluates a child, the parent wants the child to be assessed in another area. Can the district evaluate that area before the parent can request an IEE? (See OSEP Letter to Carroll, p. 37)

Is the right to examine education records limited to parents of children who have been found eligible for special education services, or does the right extend to parents of children who are suspected of having disabilities? (See OSEP Letter to Nisha Kashyap, Esq., p. 37)

Although the Individuals with Disabilities Education Act was last reauthorized in 2004, the law continues to evolve. As you study the decisions, policy guidance, publications, and special education news in ***Wrightslaw: Special Education Legal Developments and Cases 2016***, you'll realize how fast the law is evolving.

How This Book is Organized

Wrightslaw: Special Education Legal Developments and Cases 2016 is organized into four chapters.

Chapter 1 introduces legal terms and concepts. You learn about statutes, regulations, case law, judicial interpretations, and factors that cause law to evolve and change. This chapter includes an overview of the federal laws that govern the education of children with disabilities.

Chapter 2 focuses on special education legal news and developments. This chapter includes updates on lawsuits brought by the American Civil Liberties Union (ACLU) in school abuse cases and the newspaper series ***Denied,*** about how staff at a state Department of Education created a secret system to deny special education services to tens of thousands of qualified children with disabilities for over a decade.

Chapter 2 includes actions taken by the Department of Justice (DOJ) and guidance from Office of Special Education and Rehabilitation Services (OSERS) and Office of Special Education Programs (OSEP) in the form of "Dear Colleague" letters and memos.

Chapter 3 begins with a Table of Decisions by the Courts of Appeals. Decisions are in chronological order from January through December 2016. The Table of Decisions includes the date, court, judge if known, and a synopsis of the legal issues. Each case in the Table of Decisions is linked to a summary of the case that includes the outcome and prevailing party. Whenever possible, the Court's words are used to describe the issues and rulings.

Chapter 4 is about utilizing Google Scholar, the free accessible search engine that indexes the full text of federal and state legal decisions. You will learn how to find decisions in your areas of interest.

If you have the e-book edition of ***Wrightslaw: Special Education Legal Developments and Cases 2016,*** we encourage you to use the "Search" and "Find" features. "Search" is a fast, easy way to find the information you need.

Wrightslaw: Special Education Legal Developments and Cases 2016 is a legal reference book. We recommend that you begin by reading the Introduction, Chapters 1, 2, and the Table of Decisions in Chapter 3. Skim the case summaries that follow the Table of Decisions. Next, read Chapter 4 and practice finding cases on Google Scholar.

After you finish the Google Scholar Tutorial, review the case summaries in Chapter 3.

In Summation

Now that you've finished the Introduction, you have a clearer sense of how this book is organized, what is included, and how you can get the most out of the book.

Let's move on to Chapter 1 about legal terms and the federal education laws that govern the education of children with disabilities.

Chapter 1

Legal Concepts and Education Laws

This chapter introduces legal terms and concepts.

You will learn about the four types of law: federal and state constitutions, statutes, regulations, and case law.

An overview of the federal laws that govern the education of children with disabilities follows. These laws include the Individuals with Disabilities Education Act (IDEA), Section 504 of the Rehabilitation Act (Section 504), Americans with Disabilities Act Amendment Act (ADA AA), Every Student Succeeds Act (ESSA), Family Educational and Rights and Privacy Act (FERPA), and McKinney-Vento Homeless Assistance Act.

Types of Law

There are four types of law: federal and state constitutions, statutes, regulations, and case law. Case law refers to judicial interpretations of statutes and regulations that cause law to evolve and change.

Constitutional Law

The United States Constitution outlines the structure of the federal government. All laws passed must agree with the principles and rights set forth in the Constitution.

The first ten amendments to the Constitution are the Bill of Rights. The Bill of Rights is the source of the most fundamental rights – freedom of speech and religion,[5] protection against unreasonable searches and seizures,[6] and protection from cruel and unusual punishment.[7]

The Fourteenth Amendment was added later, is titled "Civil Rights," but is better known as the "Equal Protection Clause."[8] These Amendments[9] were added to the Constitution to protect citizens against interference from the federal government.

States must ensure that their statutes and regulations are consistent with the United States Code (U.S.C.) and the Code of Federal Regulations (CFR). While state statutes and regulations may provide more rights than federal laws, they cannot provide fewer rights than guaranteed by federal law. If a state law or regulation is in direct conflict with a federal law, federal law controls pursuant to the "Supremacy Clause" of the U. S. Constitution.[10]

---

[5] First Amendment

[6] Fourth Amendment

[7] Eighth Amendment

[8] Fourteenth Amendment: "nor shall any State deprive any person of life, liberty, or property, without due process of law; nor deny to any person within its jurisdiction the equal protection of the laws."

[9] http://www.ushistory.org/documents/amendments.htm

[10] U. S. Constitution, Article VI, Clause 2 – "This Constitution . . . shall be the supreme law of the land; and the judges in every state shall be bound thereby . . ."

Statutes

Statutes are laws passed by federal, state, and local legislatures. The original federal special education law was the "Education for All Handicapped Children Act of 1975." This law has been reauthorized and renamed several times since 1975.

When Congress reauthorized the law in 2004, it was titled as the "Individuals with Disabilities Education Act"[11] but is commonly referred to as "IDEA 2004" to distinguish it from the earlier 1997 version, known as IDEA 97.

Regulations & Commentary

After Congress reauthorized the Individuals with Disabilities Education Act in 2004, the U.S. Department of Education (ED) developed proposed special education regulations. The ED published the proposed regulations in the *Federal Register* (F.R.) and solicited comments from citizens and stakeholders.

On August 14, 2006, the final IDEA 2004 Regulations and an Analysis of Comments and Changes (Commentary) were published in the *Federal Register.*[12]

The IDEA 2004 regulations[13] are published in Volume 34, Part 300 of the Code of Federal Regulations. The legal citation for the regulations is 34 CFR Part 300.

A regulation must be consistent with the law and may provide more details and specifics than the statute and is considered to have the "force of law."

State Law and Regulations

State constitutions establish the structure of state government. To receive federal special education funds, states must develop special education statutes and regulations that are consistent with the United States Code (U.S.C.) and the Code of Federal Regulations (CFR). State statutes and regulations may provide more rights than federal law but may not take away rights provided by federal law.

Federal Education Statutes

Several federal statutes affect the education of children with disabilities, including:

- The Individuals with Disabilities Education Act (IDEA) begins at 20 U.S.C. §1400, *et seq.*
- Section 504 of the Rehabilitation Act begins at 29 U.S.C. § 794, *et seq.*
- The Americans with Disabilities Act Amendments Act of 2008, known as ADA AA, begins at 42 USCA § 12101, *et seq.*
- The Every Student Succeeds Act of 2015 (ESSA), successor to the No Child Left Behind Act of 2001 and a reauthorization of the Elementary and Secondary Education Act of 1965 (ESEA), begins at 20 U.S.C. § 6301, *et seq.*
- The Family Educational and Rights and Privacy Act, known as FERPA, begins at 20 U.S.C. § 1232, *et seq.*
- The McKinney-Vento Homeless Assistance Act begins at 42 U.S.C. § 11431, *et seq.*

[11] 20 U.S.C. §1400(a) See *Wrightslaw: Special Education Law, 2nd ed.*, page 45.

[12] The Commentary is at http://www.wrightslaw.com/idea/commentary.htm

[13] For the IDEA regulations, see *Wrightslaw: Special Education Law, 2nd ed.*, beginning on page 187.

Individuals with Disabilities Education Act (IDEA 2004)

The most important statute in the IDEA is the "Purposes" of the law, located in Section 1400(d). The statement of Purposes is your mission statement. The primary purposes of IDEA are:

> *[To] ensure that all children with disabilities have available to them a free appropriate public education that emphasizes special education and related services designed to meet their unique needs and prepare them for further education, employment and independent living . . . [and] to ensure that the rights of children with disabilities and parents of such children are protected ...*[14]

Section 1401 of IDEA includes thirty-six legal definitions in alphabetical order. Read these definitions carefully, especially the definitions of child with a disability, free appropriate public education, related services, special education, supplementary aids and services, and transition services.[15]

Child with a Disability[16]

If you are a parent, the most important definition is likely to be "child with a disability." Your child's classification as a "child with a disability" determines whether your child is eligible for special education and related services under the law.

A child with a disability is not automatically eligible for special education and related services under IDEA. To be eligible for a free appropriate public education under the IDEA, a child must meet two criteria. The child must have a disability and, "**by reason thereof, needs special education and related services**" (emphasis added).

Over time, courts have held that the child's disability must "adversely affect" educational performance.

If a child has a disability but does not **need** "special education and related services," the child will not be eligible under IDEA but may be eligible for accommodations and protections under Section 504 of the Rehabilitation Act and the Americans with Disabilities Act (ADA).

Free Appropriate Public Education (FAPE)[17]

The term 'free appropriate public education' means special education and related services that–

(A) have been provided at public expense, under public supervision and direction, and without charge;

(B) meet the standards of the State educational agency;

(C) include an appropriate preschool, elementary school, or secondary school education in the State involved; and

(D) are provided in conformity with the individualized education program required under Section 1414(d) of this title.

In *Board of Education v. Rowley,*[18] the U.S. Supreme Court (SCOTUS) held that children with disabilities are entitled to access to an education that provides educational benefit, but are not entitled to the "best" education nor an education that would "maximize" their potential.[19]

---

[14] 20 U.S.C. §1400(d), see *Wrightslaw: Special Education Law, 2nd ed.*, page 48.

[15] 20 U.S.C. §1401, see *Wrightslaw: Special Education Law, 2nd ed.*, page 49.

[16] 20 U.S.C. §1401(3), see *Wrightslaw: Special Education Law, 2nd ed.*, page 49.

[17] 20 U.S.C. §1401(9), see *Wrightslaw: Special Education Law, 2nd ed.*, page 51.

[18] 458 U.S. 176 (1982), see *Wrightslaw: Special Education Law, 2nd ed.*, page 343.

[19] The full text of the decision in *Rowley* is in *Wrightslaw: Special Education Law, 2nd ed.*, page 343.

Special Education Legal Developments & Cases 2016

On March 22, 2017, SCOTUS issued a unanimous decision in *Endrew F. v. Douglas County Sch. Dist. RE-1*[20] that expanded the *Rowley* decision and the statutory definition of a free appropriate public education (FAPE).

Related Services

Related services are services the child needs to benefit from special education and include:

> [T]ransportation, and such developmental, corrective, and other supportive services (including speech-language pathology and audiology services, interpreting services, psychological services, physical and occupational therapy, recreation) . . . designed to enable a child with a disability . . . to benefit from special education . . . [21]

Special Education

The law defines "special education" as "specially designed instruction . . . to meet the unique needs of a child with a disability . . ."[22]

> If the child has a disability and an IEP, the school must provide physical education as part of the child's special education program.[23] Many children benefit from adapted physical education (APE). Because physical education is a required component of special education, the child's physical education teacher should be a member of the child's IEP team.[24]

Supplementary Aids and Services

The IDEA defines supplementary aids and services as:

> . . . [A]ids, services, and other supports that are provided in regular education classes, other education-related settings, and in extracurricular and nonacademic settings, to enable children with disabilities to be educated with nondisabled children [in the least restrictive environment] . . . [25]

The school must provide nonacademic and extracurricular services and activities so children with disabilities can participate in school services and activities. Supplemental services include athletics, transportation, recreational activities, special interest groups or clubs sponsored by the school, employment assistance.[26]

Transition Services

The goal of transition is to improve the child's academic and functional achievement and to facilitate the child's movement from school to employment and further education. Transition services must be based on "the individual child's needs, taking into account the child's strengths, preferences and interests."[27]

Commentary to the IDEA Regulations

---

[20] http://www.wrightslaw.com/law/caselaw/2017/ussupct.endrew.douglas.15-827.pdf

[21] 20 U.S.C. §1401(26), see *Wrightslaw: Special Education Law, 2nd ed.*, page 54.

[22] 20 U.S.C. §1401(29), see *Wrightslaw: Special Education Law, 2nd ed.*, page 55.

[23] 20 U.S.C. §1401(29)(B), see *Wrightslaw: Special Education Law, 2nd ed.*, page 55.

[24] For the legal requirements for Physical Education and Adapted Physical Education, see http://www.wrightslaw.com/info/pe.index.htm

[25] 20 U.S.C. §1401(33), see *Wrightslaw: Special Education Law, 2nd ed.*, page 55.

[26] 34 C.F.R. §300.107 – Nonacademic services, see *Wrightslaw: Special Education Law, 2nd ed.*, page 206. For U.S.C. §1401(34), see *Wrightslaw: Special Education Law, 2nd ed.*, page 56.

[27] 34 C.F.R. §300.43(a)(2), see *Wrightslaw: Special Education Law, 2nd ed.*, page 203.

When the Department of Education published the Regulations for IDEA 2004, they included an "Analysis of Comments and Changes," also known as the "Commentary."[28] The Commentary describes terms, definitions, and requirements in clear language.[29]

When you are wrestling with the meaning of a regulation, read the discussion about that regulation in the Commentary. The Commentary will help you understand the decision to write the regulation as it is. The Commentary will also help you understand different perspectives on a specific regulation.

Section 504 of the Rehabilitation Act of 1973

Section 504 of the Rehabilitation Act is a civil rights law that prohibits discrimination against individuals with disabilities. Section 504 is intended to ensure that children with disabilities have equal access to education. The Purposes of Section 504 are:

> "To empower individuals with disabilities to maximize employment, economic self- sufficiency, independence, and inclusion and integration into society . . . No otherwise qualified individual with a disability in the United States . . . shall, solely by reason of her or his disability, be excluded from the participation in, be denied the benefits of, or be subjected to discrimination under any program or activity receiving Federal financial assistance . . ."[30]

There are significant differences between a FAPE under Section 504 and a FAPE under IDEA. A free appropriate public education (FAPE) under Section 504 requires the school to provide regular or special education aids and services that meet the child's educational needs as adequately as the needs of non-disabled students are met.[31]

A free appropriate public education (FAPE) under IDEA requires the school to provide an Individualized Education Program (IEP) that is designed to meet the child's unique needs and provide the child with educational benefit.[32]

IDEA includes an elaborate system of procedural safeguards designed to protect the child and parents. These safeguards include written notice before any change of placement and the right to an independent educational evaluation at public expense. Section 504 does not include these protections but, in some instances, provides more rights and remedies.[33]

Americans with Disabilities Act Amendments Act (ADA AA)

Congress amended the Americans with Disabilities Act (ADA) in 2008. It is known as the "ADA" and the "ADA AA," the latter "AA" referring to "Amendments Act." The 2008 amendments to ADA broadened the

---

[28] http://www.wrightslaw.com/idea/commentary.htm

[29] Download the full text of the Regulations and Commentary or specific parts such as Evaluations, IEPs, etc., from http://www.wrightslaw.com/idea/commentary.htm

[30] 20 U.S.C. §794, see *Wrightslaw: Special Education Law, 2nd ed.*, page 291.

[31] Section 504 regulations state that a "free appropriate public education [is] the provision of regular or special education and related aids and services that . . . are designed to meet individual educational needs of persons with disabilities as adequately as the needs of persons without disabilities are met." 34 CFR. § 104.33(b)(1).

[32] The *Rowley* decision is at http://www.wrightslaw.com/law/caselaw/ussupct.rowley.htm

[33] Download the excellent ***Parent and Educator Resource Guide to Section 504 in Public Elementary and Secondary Schools*** from http://wrightslaw.com/law/ocr/sec504.guide.ocr.2016.pdf
What's Your 504 IQ? Take the **504 Quiz** at http://wrightslaw.com/law/ocr/sec504.quiz.pdf

definition of disability.[34] Section 504 incorporates the ADA by reference; it applies to all students who attend public schools.

The Americans with Disabilities Act (ADA) "prohibits discrimination against individuals with disabilities in State and local government services, on the basis of disability by state and local governments, public accommodations, transportation and telecommunications."[35]

Title II of the ADA states: "No qualified individual with a disability shall, by reason such disability, be excluded from participation in or be denied the benefits of the services, programs, or activities of a public entity, or be subjected to discrimination by any such entity."[36]

Wrightslaw note: Section 504 is codified at 29 U.S.C. § 794. Implementing regulations are at Part 104 and 34 CFR. Title II of the ADA is codified at 42 U.S.C. § 12131- 12132. Implementing regulations are at 28 CFR. Part 35. Title III of the ADA about public accommodations including private, non-religious schools is at 42 U.S.C. §§ 12182-12182(b)(1)(E). Implementing regulations are at 28 CFR Part 36.

Every Student Succeeds Act of 2015 (ESSA)

In December 2015, the No Child Left Behind Act of 2001 (NCLB) was replaced by the "Every Student Succeeds Act (ESSA). NCLB and the ESSA are new versions of the original Elementary and Secondary Education Act of 1965 (ESEA) which begins at 20 U.S.C. § 6301, *et seq.*

The purpose of the ESSA is "to provide all children significant opportunity to receive a fair equitable, and high quality education, and to close educational achievement gaps."[37]

Wrightslaw note: After the Statement of Purpose, you may be surprised when you read the list of actions that the Secretary of Education is forbidden from taking. Congress intended to reduce the federal role in education but did not reduce federal education funding.

Wrightslaw note: The Advocacy Institute has collected an impressive library of resources about ESSA.[38]

Family Education Rights and Privacy Act (FERPA)

The Family Education Rights and Privacy Act (FERPA)[39] is a federal statute with the purpose of protecting the privacy of education records. FERPA addresses issues about education records that include but are not limited to:

- Rights to inspect and review educational records
- Procedures to amend education records
- Conditions and consent for disclosure of personally identifiable information from education records
- Enforcement procedures[40]

FERPA applies to all agencies and institutions that receive federal funds, including elementary and high schools, colleges, and universities.

The FERPA statute is in the United States Code at 20 U.S.C. § 1232g and 1232h. The FERPA regulations are in the Code of Federal Regulations at 34 CFR Part 99. The FERPA regulations are written in an easy-to-

---

[34] 42 U.S.C. § 12102(4)(A) - "shall be construed in favor of broad coverage" . . . and includes disabilities that are "episodic" such as diabetes, epilepsy and allergies. (42 U.S.C. § 12102(4)(D)).

[35] ***The ADA: Your Rights as an Individual with a Disability*** at https://www.eeoc.gov/facts/ada18.html

[36] 42 U.S.C. §12132.

[37] The full text of ESSA is located on the Wrightslaw site at http://www.wrightslaw.com/essa/essa.391pages.pdf

[38] Every Student Succeeds Act Resources at http://www.advocacyinstitute.org/ESSA/index.shtml

[39] 20 U.S.C. §1232g, et. seq. See *Wrightslaw: Special Education Law, 2nd ed.,* page 307.

[40] 34 CFR § 99.31.

read Frequently Asked Question format.[41] If you have a question about a FERPA issue, you are likely to find the answer in these regulations.

McKinney-Vento Homeless Assistance Act[42]

The McKinney-Vento Homeless Assistance Act requires all school districts to ensure that each child of a homeless parent and each homeless child shall have equal access to the same free, appropriate public education as provided to children and youth who are not homeless.

The McKinney-Vento Homeless Assistance Act includes several requirements including:

- School districts shall make decisions in the best interest of the child;
- School districts must immediately enroll homeless children, even if medical, academic and residency records are not available; and
- School districts shall not "segregate homeless children in separate schools or separate programs within a school, based on the child's status as homeless."[43]

Evolving Case Law & Judicial Interpretations

Case Law

As you read decisions in ***Wrightslaw: Special Education Legal Developments and Cases 2016***, you will see inconsistencies from one court to another. You will also see how an issue, like "Exhaustion," has evolved from decisions issued just a few years ago.

Special education litigation usually begins with a due process hearing.[44]

Within the state due process structure, there are "single-tier"[45] states and "two-tier"[46] states. In a single-tier state, after the Hearing Officer or Administrative Law Judge issues a decision, the losing party can appeal to federal or state court. In a two-tier state, the losing party must first appeal to the state department of education to have a Review Officer or Review Panel appointed. After the Review Officer issues a decision, the losing party can then appeal to federal or state court.

State courts and federal courts are different judicial systems. As a rule, after a case is filed in state or federal court, it will remain in that system. Cases filed in state court usually remain in the state court system while cases filed in federal district courts generally remain in the federal court system. Occasionally, a case in state court will be "removed" to federal court and a federal case may be remanded back to state court. Removal depends on whether a "Federal Question" is contained in the pleadings or earlier decisions.

Most appeals of Due Process and Review decisions in special education cases are filed in federal court (U. S. District Court). The losing party at the District Court level can file an appeal in their U. S. Court of Appeals. Table 1 lists the states in each appeals court.

A Court of Appeals panel consists of three judges. After a decision is issued, the losing party may ask the U. S. Supreme Court to hear the case.

Before appealing to the Supreme Court, the losing party may petition the Court of Appeals for an En Banc hearing, i.e., a hearing before the full panel of all Court of Appeals judges. The basis to request an En Banc

---

[41] http://www.ecfr.gov/cgi-bin/text-idx?rgn=div5&node=34:1.1.1.1.33

[42] 42 U.S.C. §11431, et. seq., see *Wrightslaw: Special Education Law, 2nd ed.*, page 319.

[43] 42 U.S.C. §11432(e)(3).

[44] 20 U.S.C. §1415(f) see *Wrightslaw: Special Education Law, 2nd ed.*, page 112.

[45] 20 U.S.C. §1415(i) see *Wrightslaw: Special Education Law, 2nd ed.*, page 115.

[46] 20 U.S.C. §1415(g) see *Wrightslaw: Special Education Law, 2nd ed.*, page 116. 40 FRAP 35(b)(1)(A).

hearing is that the "panel decision conflicts with a decision of the U. S. Supreme Court or of [that circuit] court . . . and consideration by the full court is therefore necessary to secure and maintain uniformity of the court's decisions . . ."[47]

Legal Interpretations

Law is subject to different interpretations. If you read an article about a special education decision, the interpretations and conclusions in that article will reflect the opinions and biases of the author. If you read the case on your own, your interpretations and conclusions of the case may be quite different. This is why it is so important for you to read cases, statutes, and regulations yourself, instead of relying on the opinions of others.

When a case has compelling facts, the judge(s) may write a decision that is contrary to the current case law in that Circuit. To support this decision, the judge may find and use unique facts within the case or a loophole in the law to create an "exception to the general rule." Decisions that are "exceptions to the general rule" cause the body of law to change and grow.

When you read an article about a changing area of law, the author may note that the "General Rule" or "Majority Rule" has been "swallowed up by the exceptions to the rule," so that the exceptions have now become the general rule.

When Congress wants to pass a law but cannot agree on the wording of the law, members often compromise by using vague language in the bill. Vague words and phrases in statutes are confusing but are normal in all laws.

Confusing words and phrases lead to litigation. As you will see in ***Wrightslaw: Special Education Legal Developments and Cases 2016***, the legal definitions of an "appropriate education" and "educational benefit" are still being litigated today, decades after the U.S. Supreme Court issued their 1982 decision in *Rowley*.

When most courts agree on an interpretation, a majority rule usually evolves. A minority rule may also develop. If a majority rule does not develop, the legal issue becomes more confusing with conflicting rulings from different courts on the same issue.

As happened in *Florence County School District IV v. Shannon Carter*, 501 U.S. 7,[48] Courts of Appeal in different circuits issue conflicting rulings. Conflicting rulings lead to "splits between circuits."

The U.S. Supreme Court often declines to accept a case for Certiorari unless there is a split between circuits that needs to be resolved.

---

[47] FRAP 35(b)(1)(A).

[48] *Florence County Sch. Dist. IV v. Carter*, 510 US 7 (1993) is at http://www.wrightslaw.com/law/caselaw/ussupct.carter.htm; also in *Wrightslaw: Special Education Law, 2nd ed.*, beginning on page 382.

U. S. Courts of Appeal - Twelve Circuits

As you see in the Table below, each state and territory is in one of twelve circuits. What Circuit is your state in?

Table	States in Each Circuit
1st Circuit	MA, ME, NH, RI, PR
2nd Circuit	CT, NY, VT
3rd Circuit	DE, NJ, PA, USVI
4th Circuit	MD, NC, SC, VA, WV
5th Circuit	LA, MS, TX
6th Circuit	KY, MI, OH TN
7th Circuit	IL, IN, WI
8th Circuit	AR, IA, MN, MO, ND, NE, SD
9th Circuit	AK, AZ, CA, HI, ID, MT, NV, OR, WA
10th Circuit	CO, KS, NM, OK, UT, WY
11th Circuit	AL, FL, GA
DC Circuit	Washington, DC

When a federal judge in your state issues a decision that provides a new definition or legal standard, that decision is binding on all district courts in your state, but it is not binding on federal judges in other states.

When a three-judge panel in a Court of Appeals issues a decision on a new standard or legal definition, that ruling is binding on all federal district courts within that circuit but it is not binding on federal courts in other circuits. That decision may, however, be considered "persuasive authority."[49]

It is not unusual for one circuit to issue a ruling that is in direct conflict with another circuit, i.e., a "split between circuits." That's what happened in the author's *Carter* case. The Fourth Circuit issued a ruling[50] that conflicted with an earlier ruling from the Second Circuit.

Previously, the Second Circuit issued a decision in *Tucker v. Bay Shore Union Free School District.*[51] *Tucker* held that parents could not be reimbursed for private school tuition, even if the public school's IEP was not appropriate, if the private program was not on the state's approved list and the teachers were not certified or licensed by the state.

In *Carter*, the Fourth Circuit held that reimbursement is proper if the private program is appropriate, even if the program is not on the state's approved list and the teachers are not certified by the state. The Supreme Court upheld the Fourth Circuit's decision.

---

[49] https://www.law.georgetown.edu/academics/academic-programs/legal-writing-scholarship/writing-center/upload/secondarysources.pdf

[50] *Carter v. Florence County Sch. Dist. IV*, 950 F.2d 156 (4th Cir. 1991) is at http://www.wrightslaw.com/law/caselaw/case_carter_4cir.htm

[51] *Tucker v. Bay Shore Union Free School District*, 873 F.2d 563 (2d Cir. 1989).

Split Between Circuits / U. S. Supreme Court Appeal

When two Circuits issue decisions that conflict with each other on the same legal issue, this is known as a "Split Between Circuits" or a "Circuit Split." Typically, the Supreme Court of the United States (SCOTUS) does not hear a case unless there is a split between circuits or a significant issue of public policy.

> "A Petition for a Writ of Certiorari is rarely granted when the asserted error consists of erroneous factual findings or the misapplication of a properly stated rule of law." See Rule 10 of the *Rules of the Supreme Court of the United States.*[52]

When the U. S. Supreme Court issues a ruling, pursuant to the *Supremacy Clause* of the U. S. Constitution, it becomes the "law of the land" and is binding throughout the country.

Legal Research

When you are researching a legal issue, you need to study:

- United States Code, i.e., the Statute
- Federal Regulations, the "Commentary," State Regulations and State Law
- Judicial decisions, also known as case law

When you have a question about a legal issue, read the United States Code section about your issue first. Check the footnotes at the bottom of ***Wrightslaw: Special Education Law, 2nd Edition*** to see if we discussed that statute. Next, read the federal regulation about the issue. Then, read the Commentary to the Regulations to get a clearer sense of disputed issues in the regulation. You should expect to read the statute and regulation more than once.

After you understand the federal law and regulation, read your state special education statute and regulation. In many instances, you will find that your state laws / regulations are a verbatim "copy and paste" of the federal law . . . but not always. Note any differences between federal and state law. Most states have very few special education statutes, with the bulk of state law contained in the state regulations.

When you find cases about your issue, read the earlier decisions first, before reading recent decisions. If you know a case was appealed, read the earlier decision that was appealed and reversed or affirmed. When you read early decisions first, you will have a clearer sense of how the law on this issue is evolving. You will be in a stronger position to predict the evolution of that legal issue.[53]

When one court takes a position that the law is clear, another court may interpret the law differently and arrive at a different opinion. This is the nature of law.

Legal Citations - U.S.C. / F.3d

References to law are called legal citations. Legal citations are standardized formats that explain where you will find a statute, regulation or case. When you see a legal citation such as 20 U.S.C. § 1400 *et seq.*, the term "*et seq.*" means beginning in Volume 20 of the United States Code at Section 1400 and continuing thereafter.[54]

In the United States Code, the "Findings and Purposes" of the IDEA are in Section 1400 of Title 20. The legal citation for Findings and Purposes is 20 U.S.C. § 1400. You may refer to Findings and Purposes as "20 U.S.C. § 1400" or "Section 1400."

---

[52] http://www.supremecourt.gov/ctrules/2013RulesoftheCourt.pdf

[53] For example, a split between circuits developed about the term, "educational benefit." Does it mean "some educational benefit" or "meaningful educational benefit?" Some courts held that Congress raised the *Rowley* standard while other courts disagreed.

[54] In Latin, *et seq.* is "et sequentes," which means "and the following." The term is italicized and there is no period after et

Legal decisions issued by the Courts of Appeal are published in the *Federal Reporter, Third Edition.* These decisions are cited as volume number, F.3d, followed by page number, with the Circuit and year in parentheses.

Decisions in the first edition of the *Federal Reporter,* published between 1825 and 1925, are cited as F.1d. Decisions issued between 1925 and 1993 were published in F.2d. In 1993, the first edition of F.3d was published. The third edition of the *Federal Reporter* for the Courts of Appeal is nearing volume 850. In a few years, after publication of 999 F.3, legal citations will change to the Fourth Edition.

Many cases in ***Wrightslaw: Special Education Legal Developments and Cases 2016*** will not be published in the *Federal Reporter, Third Edition,* so there will be no "F.3d" legal citation for those cases. Later, a few cases that do not currently have a F.3d citation may be published in F.3d. If the "F.3d" citation is available when this book is published, we will include that citation with the case.

When a Court of Appeals believes that a decision is not noteworthy or does not create new law, that case is not recommended for publication in the *Federal Reporter,* i.e., F.3d.

Wrightslaw: Special Education Legal Developments and Cases 2016 includes most Court of Appeals cases issued in 2016. The Court of Appeals decisions that were not included are short (usually one-page) rulings with no significant information about the facts and legal issues.

The first two cases listed in the Table of Cases in Chapter 3 are not published in the *Federal Reporter.* The third case was published in in the *Federal Reporter* and is cited as 810 F.3d 961 (5th Cir. 2016). This means that the decision was published in Volume 810 of F.3d, beginning at page 961 and was issued by the Fifth Circuit in 2016.

Do Not Publish / FRAP 32.1

As you read these cases, you may notice a statement at the beginning such as "Not Precedential" or "Do Not Publish" or "Not for Publication." This does not mean that you cannot publish the decision or that you cannot rely on the decision as law.

Unless a decision includes other restrictions, "Do Not Publish" usually means that, in the opinion of the judges on that panel, the decision is not noteworthy, does not create new legal precedent, and should not be published in the *Federal Reporter.*

The notation "Do Not Publish" is addressed in Rule 32.1, "Citing Judicial Dispositions" in the *Federal Rules of Appellate Procedure (FRAP).*[55]

All cases in ***Wrightslaw: Special Education Legal Developments and Cases 2016*** are available from Google Scholar, a publicly accessible electronic database, and can be disseminated. In Chapter 4, you will learn how to use Google Scholar to find the full text of all decisions in this book and many others.

Chapter 3 includes all decisions issued by the U. S. Courts of Appeal in special education cases between January 1, 2016 and December 31, 2016. The decisions are available from Google Scholar and include the terms "Individuals with Disabilities Education Act," "Section 504 of the Rehabilitation Act," and the "Americans with Disabilities Act."

In the beginning of Chapter 3, you will find a **Table of Special Education Legal Decisions in 2016.** The Table of Decisions includes the date of the decision, circuit and author of the decision, if known, the F.3d citation if known, our abbreviated "style of the case," key concepts / issues addressed in the ruling, and

---

[55] "A court may not prohibit or restrict the citation of federal judicial opinions, orders, judgments, or other written dispositions that have been designated as 'unpublished,' 'not for publication,' 'non-precedential,' 'not precedent,' or the like; [and that] if a party cites a federal judicial opinion, order, judgment, or other written disposition that is not available in a publicly accessible electronic database, the party must file and serve a copy of that opinion, order, judgment, or disposition with the brief or other paper in which it is cited." (FRAP 32.1)

outcome. After the Table of Decisions is Table of Cases listed alphabetically and hyperlinked so you can jump quickly to a case.

Some decisions do not include an author. Court of Appeals decisions that are one or two paragraph "summaries" that provide minimal detail and minimal law were omitted from this book.

Each case in the Table of Decisions is bookmarked to a thorough discussion of the case. In general, we used the Court's words to describe the facts, findings, and rulings.

As you review Chapter 3, you may want to focus on decisions from your circuit.

In Summation

In this chapter, you learned about statutes, regulations, case law, judicial interpretations, and how law evolves. You also learned about legal research and legal citations.

In the next chapter, you will dive into legal news, developments, and cases.

Chapter 2

Special Education Legal News and Developments

Chapter 2 includes news and developing areas of special education law.

2016 was a remarkable year in special education law. The U. S. Supreme Court granted certiorari in two special education cases. You will learn about the **2016 Cases of the Year** and what made these cases unique. You'll learn about discrimination cases initiated and settled by the Department of Justice (DOJ) and cases brought in school abuse cases brought by the America Civil Liberties Union.

On the News front, you'll learn about ***Denied,*** a series of articles by an investigative journalist that describe how unelected state employees in Texas created a secret cap on the percentage of children with disabilities who could receive special education and related services. This secret system caused tens of thousands of qualified children with disabilities to be denied services and operated for almost fifteen years. After learning about this system, parents and advocates around the country lost trust that the system would protect their children's rights.

This chapter includes all guidance letters, memos, and publications published by the Office of Special Education and Rehabilitation Services (OSERS), Office of Special Education Programs (OSEP), and Office for Civil Rights (OCR) in 2016.

Special Education News

When the U. S. Supreme Court issues decisions in the two special education cases, this lays the groundwork for significant changes in how the law is implemented.

When you read the articles in ***Denied***, the series by journalist Brian M. Rosenfeld, and learn how the secret system and cap became public knowledge, you may ask,

"Does my state have a system to deny services to qualified children?"

"What will happen to the thousands of children who were illegally denied special education and related services?"

"Who enforces the Individuals with Disabilities Education Act?

"Who can we trust?"

Chapter 2 of ***Wrightslaw: Special Education Legal Developments and Cases 2016*** includes recent guidance letters, memos, and publications from the Office of Special Education and Rehabilitation Services (OSERS), Office of Special Education Programs (OSEP) and Office for Civil Rights (OCR).

Cases of the Year for 2016

The **2016 Cases of the Year** are:

AG v. Paradise Valley Unified School District, 815 F.3d 1195 (9th Cir. 2016)

Timothy O. v. Paso Robles Unified School District, 822 F.3d 1105 (9th Cir. 2016)

LO v. NYC DOE, 822 F.3d 95 (2nd Cir. 2016)

Cobb County Sch. Dist. v. DB (11th Cir. 2016)

AG v. Paradise Valley Unified. Sch. Dist., 815 F.3d 1195 (9th Cir. 2016) is about a school district's failure to provide adequate accommodations and the district's decision to change a child's placement. The Court of Appeals held that FAPE under IDEA is different from FAPE under Section 504 / ADA.

In ***Timothy O. v. Paso Robles Unified School District***, 822 F.3d 1105 (9th Cir. 2016), a school district determined that a child with autism was not eligible for special education services. The eligibility decision was based on the opinion of a school psychologist who did not evaluate the child.

LO v. NYC DOE, 822 F.3d 95 (2nd Cir. 2016) includes procedural and substantive violations of IDEA. The violations included failure to conduct Functional Behavior Assessments and create Behavior Intervention Plans, failure to review evaluation materials before developing the child's IEPs, failure to develop IEP goals that met the child's needs, and other errors and omissions. The Court ordered relief that extended beyond the student's 22nd birthday.

Cobb County Sch. Dist. v. DB (11th Cir. 2016) is a case about independent educational evaluations (IEEs) and attorney's fees. The Court of Appeals vacated the district court's decision to reduce the parents' fee award from nearly $300,000 to $75,000 after finding that "the State or local educational agency unreasonably protracted the final resolution of the action or proceeding."

Supreme Court Grants Certiorari in Two Special Ed Cases

In 2016, the Supreme Court of the United States (SCOTUS) granted certiorari in two cases: *Fry v. Napoleon* (6th Circuit) and *Endrew F. v. Douglas Co. Sch. Dist. RE-1* (10th Circuit).

The primary legal issue in *Fry v. Napoleon* was exhaustion of administrative remedies. The IDEA requires that parties request a due process hearing before filing suit in Court. In 2015, cases brought under Section 504/ADA - not IDEA - were dismissed in the 3rd, 6th, 9th, 10th, and 11th Circuits. In some of the cases dismissed, the children had never been found eligible for special education under IDEA or the relief they sought was not available under the IDEA.[56]

The primary legal issue in *Endrew F.* was the role of progress in a free appropriate public education. The Court first addressed this issue in *Hendrick Hudson District Bd. of Ed. v. Amy Rowley, 458 U.S. 176* (1982).[57]

In early 2017, the Supreme Court issued unanimous decisions in *Fry* and *Endrew F.*

Update on Service Dog Cases

In ***Wrightslaw: Special Education Legal Developments and Cases 2015***, service dog cases were front and center.

In 2016, the U. S. Supreme Court agreed to hear *Fry v. Napoleon*, a case about a child who needed her service dog as an accommodation at school. When the school refused to allow the dog to accompany the child and negotiations failed, the parents had to withdraw their child from her public school and enroll her in a different school district.

---

[56] *Wrightslaw: Special Education Legal Developments and Cases 2015,* pages 21-25.

[57] http://www.wrightslaw.com/law/caselaw/ussupct.rowley.htm

U. S. v. Gates Chili Central Sch. Dist. (W.D. NY 2016)[58] is about an eight-year-old child with autism who also has seizures. With help from her service dog, she is safer and more independent at school. As an eight-year-old, she still needs help from adults in some areas, including tasks related to her service dog. Her school district refused to provide help and required her parent to hire a certified dog handler.[59]

In ***Child with a Disability v. Sachem Central Sch. Dist. Bd. of Ed; Sachem Central Sch. Dist., and James Nolan, Superintendent*** (E.D. NY 2016),[60] a 12-year-old child with a disability and his parents allege that his school district violated Title II of the ADA by refusing to allow the child's service animal to accompany him at school or to school-related functions.

The United States submitted a Statement of Interest (SOI) to clarify the correct interpretation of Title II of the ADA with respect to the service dog issues raised by the Board of Education, School District, and superintendent.

Denied! How Texas Keeps Tens of Thousands of Children Out of Special Education

On September 9, 2016, a story broke in Texas that rocked the world of special education far beyond that state's boundaries.

Denied was the first in a series of articles written by investigative reporter Brian M. Rosenthal and published in the ***Houston Chronicle***.

Acting on a tip from an advocate, Mr. Rosenthal made a startling discovery. In 2004, about 12% of students received special education and related services in Texas. This percentage was consistent with the percentage of students who received special education in other states.

But in 2004, unelected officials at the Texas Education Agency (TEA) moved the goal posts. They reduced the percentage of students with disabilities who could receive special education, from 12% – to **8.5%**.

The Texas Education Agency pressured districts to comply by auditing districts that "served too many kids." Over the next decade, the number of children who received special education declined – to 8.5%. Not surprisingly, this plan saved Texas billions of dollars.

The Texas Legislature did not approve the cap. The state Board of Education didn't discuss the cap. Parents and the federal Department of Education didn't know about the cap.

After the Texas Education Agency implemented the 8.5% cap, tens of thousands of children with disabilities were denied special education services and a free appropriate public education. This story is still unfolding.

The articles in **Denied** describe what happened to children with disabilities and their families after the secret cap was imposed. The stories are enlightening but often heart-breaking.

1. ***Denied. How Texas quietly keeps tens of thousands of children out of special education.***[61]
2. ***Schools push students out of special education to meet state limit.***[62]
3. ***Mentally ill lose out as special ed declines.***[63]
4. ***Facing pressure to cut special ed, Texas schools shut out English Language Learners.***[64]

[58] https://www.ada.gov/gateschili/gates-chili_msj.pdf

[59] *Wrightslaw: Special Education Legal Developments and Cases 2015*, page 30.

[60] https://www.ada.gov/briefs/sachem_soi.pdf

[61] http://www.houstonchronicle.com/denied/1/

[62] http://www.houstonchronicle.com/denied/2/

[63] http://www.houstonchronicle.com/denied/3/

[64] http://www.houstonchronicle.com/denied/4/

5. ***Unable to get special education in Texas, one family called it quits and moved to Pennsylvania.***[65]
6. ***Houston schools block disabled kids from special education.***[66]
7. ***Special ed cap drives families out of public schools.***[67]
8. ***Explainer: How we know the reason for the drop in special ed students.***[68]

Within hours after the first article in the **Denied**! series was published, the special education world reacted with shock and anger. Parents in other states were afraid that their states and school districts had covertly implemented similar practices. People who read these articles had questions that could not be easily answered.

How can a state improperly deny special education and related services to tens of thousands of children who are legally entitled to these services? How can these children be located? How can they be compensated for what the state denied them?

The purpose of special education is to prepare children with disabilities "**for further education, employment, and independent living** . . ."[69] How many children with disabilities in Texas were not prepared for further education, employment and independent living because they did not receive the special education and related services they needed? What can be done to help these children, many of whom are now adults?

How could the Texas legislature and the federal Department of Education be unaware of this cap for over a decade?

The over-riding questions were these: **Who is responsible for enforcing the IDEA? How will they fix this?**

Discrimination Cases under ADA and Section 504

The Department of Justice reached settlements with several YMCAs and a residential camp that refused to allow children with disabilities to participate in afterschool or summer programs and a Montessori School that refused to admit or allow children with disabilities to remain in their school.

Discrimination Against Children with Diabetes

U. S. v. Arlington-Mansfield YMCA.[70] On February 24, 2016, the Department of Justice (DOJ) reached an agreement with the Arlington-Mansfield Area YMCA, resolving allegations that it violated the Americans with Disabilities Act by refusing to admit a six-year-old child with Type I diabetes to a summer day camp program. The YMCA agreed to submit its written policies and procedures to the DOJ for review and approval and agreed to designate and maintain a compliance officer to monitor compliance with the settlement agreement.

U. S. v. Philadelphia Freedom Valley YMCA—Rocky Run Branch.[71] On May 19, 2016, the Department of Justice reached a similar agreement with the Philadelphia Freedom Valley YMCA- Rocky Run Branch. The child, with adult supervision, could monitor her blood glucose levels and administer insulin via her pump. Her parents offered to train the YMCA staff to administer glucagon; recognize signs and symptoms of low and high blood glucose levels; and supervise their child in administering insulin and counting carbohydrates.

---

[65] http://www.houstonchronicle.com/denied/5/

[66] http://www.houstonchronicle.com/denied/6/

[67] http://www.houstonchronicle.com/denied/7/

[68] http://www.houstonchronicle.com/denied/beyond-the-data/

[69] 20 U.S.C. 1400(d); page 48 in *Wrightslaw: Special Education Law, 2nd edition*

[70] https://www.ada.gov/arlington_ymca.html

[71] https://www.ada.gov/rocky_run_sa.html

U. S. v. YMCA of the Triangle.[72] On July 28, 2016, the Department of Justice reached a similar agreement with a North Carolina YMCA, resolving allegations that it violated the Americans with Disabilities Act (ADA) by refusing to allow a child with Type 1 diabetes to participate in an after-school program.

U. S. v. Camp Treetops.[73] On November 7, 2016, the Department of Justice reached an agreement with Camp Treetops, a residential summer camp in New York. In 2014, Camp Treetops informed a child's parent that its acceptance of her child into Camp Treetops' 7-week junior camp was rescinded because it learned that L.F. had Type 1 diabetes. The camp agreed to evaluate, on a case-by-case basis, and make reasonable modifications for children with disabilities, including children with diabetes who apply to be campers at Camp Treetops.

Discrimination Against Students with Disabilities: U. S. v. Ruffing Montessori School

U. S. v. Ruffing Montessori School.[74] This case is about MD, an eleven-year-old with autism. In the Spring of 2014, his mother asked a school administrator if the school would apply for an Ohio program that provides scholarships for students with special needs. In declining, the administrator wrote "... to participate, the school would have to sign an affidavit saying it 'will not discriminate based on disability and that would be tough to do.'"

In Spring 2015, the school completed a Service Plan that described the modifications the school would provide for MD in fifth grade. In late May, the administrator called to advise MD's mother that he could not return in the Fall because "the class size was too large to accommodate his needs." Because it was late in the school year, MD's mother had great difficulty finding a program that was appropriate for her son and his brother. Ultimately, she had to relocate to another city.

Under the settlement agreement, the school agreed to change its policies to ensure that students with disabilities would receive reasonable accommodations. The school also agreed to pay $45,000 in damages to three families whose children were kicked out of the school because they had disabilities.

Discrimination Against Children with Behavior-Related Disabilities: U. S. v. Georgia

On August 23, 2016, the Justice Department filed a Complaint in federal court against Georgia for running a network of "psychoeducational" schools called Georgia Network for Educational and Therapeutic Support Program (GNETS). The Complaint alleged that the State of Georgia discriminated against thousands of public school students with behavior-related disabilities by unnecessarily segregating them in a separate and unequal educational program which is financed, operated, and administered by the State.[75]
SC DOE's Failure to Maintain Financial Support for Special Education

On August 25, 2016, the Department of Education reached an agreement[76] with the South Carolina Department of Education to settle litigation about South Carolina's failure to maintain financial support for special education and related services.[77]

---

[72] https://www.ada.gov/ymca_triangle_sa.html

[73] https://www.ada.gov/camp_treetops_sa.html

[74] https://www.ada.gov/briefs/ruffing_motion_intervene.html

[75] https://www.ada.gov/olmstead/documents/gnets_complaint.html

[76] https://www2.ed.gov/policy/speced/guid/idea/memosdcltrs/south-carolina-idea-mfs-settlement-agreement.pdf

[77] https://www.ed.gov/news/press-releases/us-department-education-reaches-settlement-south-carolina-department-education-funding-children-disabilities

Language-Based Discrimination: T.R. v. The School District of Philadelphia

On January 25, 2016, the Department of Justice filed a brief with the District Court in ***T.R. v. The School District of Philadelphia***, a case about language-based discrimination. This case involves requirements for translating children's education records, especially IEPs, so their Limited English Proficient parents have meaningful access to information about their children's education and can participate in educational decision-making.[78]

South Carolina's Statewide School-to-Pipeline Case: Kenny et al. v. Wilson et al.

On November 29, 2016, the Justice Department filed a Statement of Interest in ***Kenny et al. v. Wilson et al.***, South Carolina's Statewide School-to-Pipeline case. The SOI described the position of the United States that laws invoked to charge juveniles must include clear standards to ensure that they are enforced consistently and free from discrimination.[79]

The statement explained that vague statutes contribute to the "school-to-prison pipeline," the cycle of harsh school discipline that brings young people into the justice system and disproportionately affects, among others, students of color and students with disabilities.

ACLU Files Lawsuits on Behalf of Children with Disabilities

The American Civil Liberties Association (ACLU) continued to file lawsuits on behalf of children with disabilities who are abused and injured at school. The ACLU's position is clear: if schools continue to use law enforcement officers, they must ensure that these officers are **trained to work with children with disabilities**.

In 2016, the ACLU was actively involved in cases like these and in other discrimination cases.

Seven-year-old handcuffed for crying. In 2016, a School Resource Officer handcuffed a seven-year-old child for crying in class. The child was less than four feet tall and weighed less than 50 pounds. The child has a hearing impairment and was frequently bullied by other students.[80] On September 8, 2016, the ACLU filed a lawsuit against Kansas City Schools and Brandon Craddock (SRO) for unlawfully restraining and handcuffing the K.W.P. "with excessive force and without necessity."[81]

Six-year-old child with autism beaten with 1" thick paddle. In March 2016, Landon was a six-year-old first grader with autism. An assistant principal administered an "approved punishment;" he struck this child on his bottom with an inch-thick paddle. The incident terrified the child so severely that that he had to be sedated by ambulance workers. The child was traumatized and could not return to that school. His grandmother withdrew Landon from the school, fearing for his physical and mental health, despite threats from school truancy officers that she could go to jail.[82]

School attempts to expel 10-year old for throwing toilet paper. After a ten-year-old girl with special needs was accused of throwing toilet paper, a police officer dragged her into the principal's office and placed her in handcuffs. The child panicked, struggled, and allegedly kicked the officer. The child was accused of assaulting school personnel and recommended for expulsion.

Counsel from the ACLU of Michigan attended the expulsion hearing. He persuaded the hearing officer not to expel the child because she would not be allowed to enroll in any school in the state.[83]

---

[78] https://www2.ed.gov/policy/speced/guid/idea/memosdcltrs/attachment-to-06-14-2016-email.pdf

[79] https://www.justice.gov/opa/pr/department-justice-files-statement-interest-south-carolina-statewide-school-prison-pipeline

[80] https://www.aclu-mo.org/newsviews/2016/09/08/aclu-missouri-sues-kc-public-schools-handcuffing-second-grader/

[81] https://www.aclu-mo.org/files/4814/7335/2199/PrimmVKCPS_Complaint.pdf

[82] http://www.greatschools.org/gk/articles/abuse-of-kids-with-disabilities/

[83] http://www.aclumich.org/article/attempted-expulsion-ten-year-old

In September 2016, Education Secretary John King expressed concerns about the proliferation of law enforcement officers in public schools. He clarified limits on the role of SROs: "**SROs should have no role in administering school discipline.**" (emphasis added) because of the "potential for violations of students' civil rights and unnecessary citations or arrests of students in schools, which may lead to the unnecessary, harmful introduction of children and young adults into a school-to-prison pipeline."

Policy Letters, Memos, and Dear Colleague Letters from OSERS, OSEP, & OCR

Three agencies within the U. S. Department of Education develop and interpret special education policies and guidance on how the law is administered: The Office of Special Education and Rehabilitation Services (OSERS), the Office of Special Education Programs (OSEP), and the Department of Education's Office for Civil Rights (OCR).

In 2016, these agencies issued guidance on ADHD and Section 504, behavior supports for children with disabilities, the rights of children with disabilities in public charter schools under IDEA and Section 504 of the Rehabilitation Act, restraint and seclusion, accountability of virtual schools, and the prevention of racial discrimination in special education. You can use these publications to educate school administrators and staff.

Office of Special Education and Rehabilitative Services (OSERS)

The Office of Special Education and Rehabilitative Services (OSERS)[84] focuses on improving results and outcomes for people with disabilities. OSERS supports programs that serve millions of children and adults with disabilities and monitors special education laws and regulations.

OSERS includes the Office of Special Education Programs (OSEP), and the Rehabilitation Services Administration (RSA).

Office of Special Education Programs (OSEP)

The mission of the Office of Special Education Programs (OSEP)[85] is to help States implement the Individuals with Disabilities Education Act (IDEA). OSEP develops and disseminates Federal policies on special education and related services to children with disabilities and early intervention services. OSEP also issues Policy Letters in response to questions about the Individuals with Disabilities Education Act (IDEA).

Office for Civil Rights (OCR)

The Department of Education's Office for Civil Rights (OCR)[86] investigates discrimination complaints and enforces anti-discrimination laws, including Section 504 of the Rehabilitation Act (Section 504) and the Americans with Disabilities Amendment Act of 2008 (ADA AA). These laws prohibit disability discrimination and require school districts to provide equal educational opportunities to students with disabilities.

---

[84] https://www2.ed.gov/about/offices/list/osers/osep/osep-idea.html

[85] https://www2.ed.gov/about/offices/list/osers/osep/index.html

[86] https://www2.ed.gov/about/offices/list/ocr/index.html

Guidance, Policy Memos, and Publications from OSEP & OSERS

Children with Disabilities in Nursing Homes (Joint Policy letter OSEP and OSERS, April 28, 2016)[87]

"Although the number of children who reside in nursing homes is small, their medically complex conditions present unique challenges. These children live away from their families and often stay in nursing homes for months or years."

"In 2014, the U.S. Government Accountability Office (GAO) published a report that described the unique educational challenges of serving this population.[88] The report described the responsibilities of states, school districts, and other public agencies in addressing the educational needs of children with disabilities who live in nursing homes."

"This Joint Policy letter clarifies that children with disabilities who reside in nursing homes and their parents have the same rights under IDEA that apply to other IDEA-eligible children . . . [and] identifies best practices to help States and public agencies in meeting the unique educational needs of these children."

Response to Intervention (RTI) Cannot Be Used to Delay or Deny an Evaluation for Preschool Special Education Services Under the IDEA (OSEP Memorandum 16-07, April 29, 2016)[89]

"The Child Find provision in the IDEA requires schools to evaluate and identify preschool children with disabilities in a timely manner. States and LEAs cannot have Response to Intervention procedures or practices that delay or deny this identification. States and LEAs have an obligation to ensure all children suspected of having a disability, including 3-, 4-, and 5- year-olds in preschool programs are evaluated, not delayed or denied while the school implements RTI."

Persistent Gaps in Discipline, Restraint and Seclusion, Retention, Access to Early Learning and Rigorous Courses (Civil Rights Survey, Office for Civil Rights, June 7, 2016)[90]

In June, the U.S. Department of Education's Office for Civil Rights (OCR) released data from the first annual Civil Rights Data Survey. The data showed wide gaps in areas that affect educational equity and opportunity for students. These gaps include incidents of discipline, restraint and seclusion, access to courses and programs that lead to college and career readiness, teacher equity, rates of retention, and access to early learning.[91]

Data Show Widespread Chronic Absenteeism Among All Student Groups (Civil Rights Survey, ED, June 10, 2016, updated on August 10, 2016)[92]

Data from the Civil Rights Survey revealed that more than 6 million students – 13 percent of all students – were chronically absent (defined as missing at least three weeks of school) in the 2013-2014 school year. Most children who are chronically absent have low academic achievement and are more likely to drop out of school. Data from this Survey shows that chronic absenteeism affects students in all parts of the country and among all races, gender, ages, and students with disabilities.

---

[87] https://www2.ed.gov/policy/speced/guid/idea/memosdcltrs/dcl-children-in-nursing-homes-04-28-2016.pdf

[88] Unique Challenges of Educating Children in Nursing Homes (GAO 14-585) is at http://www.gao.gov/products/GAO-14-585

[89] https://www2.ed.gov/policy/speced/guid/idea/memosdcltrs/oseprtipreschoolmemo4-29-16.pdf

[90] https://www.ed.gov/news/press-releases/persistent-disparities-found-through-comprehensive-civil-rights-survey-underscore-need-continued-focus-equity-king-says

[91] https://www.ed.gov/news/press-releases/persistent-disparities-found-through-comprehensive-civil-rights-survey-underscore-need-continued-focus-equity-king-says

[92] https://www.ed.gov/news/press-releases/new-data-show-chronic-absenteeism-widespread-and-prevalent-among-all-student-groups

IEPs of Children with Disabilities Must be Translated for Limited English Proficient (LEP) Parents (OSEP, June 14, 2016)[93]

"Given the critical role parents play in seeking and securing educational opportunities for their children, a district's failure to overcome the language barriers of an LEP parent through free translation and oral interpretation denies the child an equal educational opportunity because of national origin."

"LEP parents must be given a meaningful opportunity to understand regular and special education documents, identify the needs of their children, monitor their educational services, and enable their children's to participate in the District's instructional programs . . . without such access, neither the parents nor the District can ensure that the language needs of English Learner students are addressed, as the EEOA requires."

Educational Stability for Children in Foster Care (Departments of Education & Health & Human Services, June 23, 2016)[94]

On June 23, 2016, the Departments of Education and Health and Human Services released joint guidance about new provisions for children in foster care.

"Children and youth in foster care represent one of the most vulnerable student groups in the nation . . . 75 percent of children in foster care made an unscheduled school change in one school year. Unplanned school changes are associated with delays in academic progress, leaving highly mobile students more likely to fall behind their less mobile peers academically."

"Data show that foster youth are more likely than their peers to experience barriers that lead to troubling outcomes, including low academic achievement, grade retention. and lower high school graduation rates. The new protections for children in foster care under ESSA apply to all children in foster care enrolled in public schools." This guidance is in the form of frequently asked questions and answers about new educational stability requirements.

Section 504 and Students with ADHD

On July 27, 2016, the Office for Civil Rights published three documents about Section 504 and Students with ADHD, as listed below. If you have a child with ADHD or you advocate for children with ADHD, these publications are required reading.

Students with ADHD & Section 504: Dear Colleague Letter (OCR, July 27, 2016)[95]

The Office for Civil Rights (OCR) published this Dear Colleague Letter (DCL) after investigating thousands of disability discrimination complaints involving students with ADHD. The DCL clarifies the school's obligations to students with disabilities, including ADHD, under Section 504 of the Rehabilitation Act.

". . . OCR found while that many teachers and administrators take appropriate action to ensure that students with ADHD receive the protections to which they are entitled under Federal law . . . many other teachers and administrators are not familiar with this disorder, or how it affects a student's ability to access a school district's program."

OCR's investigations revealed that school districts often fail to identify and evaluate students with ADHD and their failure denies a free appropriate public education (FAPE) to students who need special education or related services.

---

[93] https://www2.ed.gov/policy/speced/guid/idea/memosdcltrs/iep-translation-06-14-2016.pdf

[94] https://www2.ed.gov/policy/elsec/leg/essa/edhhsfostercarenonregulatorguide.pdf

[95] https://www2.ed.gov/about/offices/list/ocr/letters/colleague-201607-504-adhd.pdf

Special Education Legal Developments & Cases 2016

Students with ADHD and Section 504: A Resource Guide[96]

The Resource Guide provides an excellent overview of the rights of students with ADHD and describes school districts' legal obligations to evaluate and provide educational services to students with disabilities. For example, the school:

- Must evaluate a child when the child needs or is believed to need special education or related services.
- Must provide services based on the child's needs, not on generalizations about disabilities or ADHD.
- May not rely on assumption that a child who performs well academically cannot be substantially limited in major life activities, including reading, learning, writing, and thinking. In fact, a child who performs well academically may also be a person with a disability.
- Must evaluate children who have behavioral difficulties and children who seems unfocused or distractible as they may have ADHD.
- Must provide parents and guardians with due process and must allow them to appeal decisions regarding the identification, evaluation, or educational placement of their children with disabilities, including children with ADHD.

Students with ADHD: Know Your Rights (Office for Civil Rights, July 27, 2016)[97] – This two-page summary of student and parent rights under Section 504 contains useful information for any parent or older child who may have a disability.

Behavioral Intervention and Supports

Providing Behavioral Interventions & Supports to Students with Disabilities (Joint Dear Colleague Letter from OSERS and OSEP, August 1, 2016)[98]

On August 1, 2016, OSERS and OSEP published a joint "Dear Colleague Letter" about the requirements to Provide Behavioral Supports in Individualized Education Programs (IEPs) to Students with Disabilities and a two-page "Summary of Rights."

In the case of a child whose behavior impedes the child's learning or the learning of others, the IEP Team **must** consider – and, when necessary to provide FAPE, include in the IEP – the **positive behavioral interventions and supports, and other strategies, to address that behavior.** (emphasis added)

Recent data on short-term disciplinary removals suggests that many children with disabilities are not receiving appropriate behavioral interventions, supports, and other strategies in their IEPs . . .. this is concerning in light of **research about the detrimental impacts of disciplinary removals . . .**"[99] (emphasis added)

If a school fails to provide appropriate positive behavioral supports to a child with a disability who need these interventions, the school may deprive the child of a free appropriate public education (FAPE).

Wrightslaw note: This publication about providing Positive Behavioral Interventions and other supports to children with disabilities is a "must-read" for all parents, teachers, advocates, and related services providers who are struggling to get a school to help a child with a disability who has behavior problems.

---

[96] http://www.wrightslaw.com/law/ocr/sec504.guide.ocr.2016.pdf

[97] https://www2.ed.gov/about/offices/list/ocr/docs/dcl-know-rights-201607-504.pdf

[98] https://www2.ed.gov/policy/gen/guid/school-discipline/files/dcl-on-pbis-in-ieps--08-01-2016.pdf

[99] Center and the Public Policy Research Institute. (2011). *Breaking schools' rules: a statewide study of how school discipline relates to students' success and juvenile justice involvement.* Available at https://csgjusticecenter.org/youth/breaking-schools-rules-report/

Summary of Positive Behavioral Interventions and Supports (2 pages)[100]

Wrightslaw note: Never assume that members of your child's team are knowledgeable about the requirements to provide Positive Behavioral Interventions.

Take several copies of this two-page "Summary of Positive Behavioral Intervention and Supports" to IEP and other school meetings – it's a great way to educate others.

Educating Children with Disabilities Who Attend Public Virtual Schools (OSERS, August 5, 2016)[101]

This Dear Colleague guidance letter explains that education models that involve online instruction and practice have proliferated over last few years. A 'virtual school' is defined as "a public school that offers only virtual courses: instruction in which children and teachers are separated by time and/or location . . . interaction occurs via computers and/or telecommunications technologies, and the school generally 'does not have a physical facility that allows children to attend classes on-site."

"Because most children who attend virtual schools do not have face-to-face interactions and in-person contacts with a teacher or other school staff as children who attend brick and mortar schools, child find for children attending virtual schools presents unique challenges.

"The educational rights and protections afforded to children with disabilities and their parents under IDEA may not be diminished when children with disabilities attend virtual schools that are constituted as LEAs or are public schools of an LEA."

School Resource Officers (SROs) Should Have No Role in School Discipline (Key Policy Letter from Education Secretary to Chief State School Officers and Superintendents, September 9, 2016)[102]

In this Policy Letter, the Education Secretary expresses concerns about the proliferation of law enforcement officers (often known as school resource officers) in public schools.

SROs should have no role in administering school discipline (emphasis added) because of the "potential for violations of students' civil rights and unnecessary citations or arrests of students in schools, which may lead to the unnecessary, harmful introduction of children and young adults into a school-to-prison pipeline."

In ***Wrightslaw: Special Education Legal Developments and Cases 2016***, you'll read the cases of two children with disabilities from New Mexico. One was a seven-year old who shot a rubber band at a police officer; the other was a thirteen-year old who burped in class. Both children were handcuffed and taken into custody by school resource officers.

The Secretary of Education urged schools to provide their staff with training to deal with behavioral issues **through corrective, non-punitive interventions** (emphasis added) . . . educators [need] the "skills to deal with behavior and discipline issues and avoid relying on SRO-related practices that may harm young people and contribute to their involvement with the juvenile and criminal justice systems . . . and the school-to-prison pipeline."[103]

Special educators may need specialized training to deal with children with behavior disorders. These children's IEPs **must include** "a statement of the program modifications or supports for school personnel that will be provided for the child."[104]

---

[100] https://www2.ed.gov/policy/gen/guid/school-discipline/files/dcl-summary-for-stakeholders.pdf

[101] https://www2.ed.gov/policy/speced/guid/idea/memosdcltrs/dcl--virtual-schools--08-05-2016.pdf

[102] https://www2.ed.gov/policy/elsec/guid/secletter/160907.html

[103] Supportive School Discipline Initiative at http://www2.ed.gov/policy/gen/guid/school-discipline/fedefforts.htm - guidance

[104] 20 U.S.C. § 1414(d)(1)(A)(i)(IV); *Wrightslaw: Special Education Law, 2nd ed.*, page 100.

"Any approach to improving school safety, security, and discipline should focus on creating a positive school climate. These strategies can resolve students' behavioral issues without relying on SROs and will reduce detentions, suspensions, expulsions, citations, and arrests in schools."

Expanding Opportunities for Youngest Learners (Department of Education, Office of Elementary and Secondary Education, October 16, 2016)[105]

The Education Department's guidance for early learning is geared to improve the health, social-emotional, and cognitive outcomes for children from birth through third grade and "to ensure that all children, especially those with high needs, are on track to graduate from high school college and career ready."

This guidance focuses on the importance of early learning, highlights opportunities under the law to strengthen early education, and provides examples of how to support young children's success in school.

Confidentiality Requirements in Early Childhood Programs

Understanding Confidentiality Requirements in IDEA Early Childhood Programs: Frequently Asked Questions (OSERS, October 20, 2016)[106]

This publication answers frequently asked questions about privacy and confidentiality under the Individuals with Disabilities Education Act (IDEA) and is intended to help early childhood providers and programs.

Questions include confidentiality under IDEA and FERPA, protection of personally identifiable information (PII), education records and early intervention records, parental consent, the right to prior written consent under FERPA, exceptions to consent, IDEA requirements for notifications to parents, duty to maintain and provisions for destruction of records, and more.

This publication can be used with the side-by-side guide, **IDEA and Family Educational Rights and Privacy Act (FERPA) Confidentiality Provisions** (2014).[107]

Meeting the Needs of Families with Children at Risk of Homelessness: Joint Policy Statement: Departments of Health and Human Services (HHS), Housing and Urban Development (HUD), and Education (ED), October 31, 2016.[108]

The most common ages to be homeless are from infancy to age five so difficulties begin early for young children from homeless families. These children's feelings of safety and security are affected by hunger, homelessness, violence, and lack of parental attention. Homelessness is a complicated and persistent problem.

This Joint Statement recommends ways that early childhood and housing providers at local and state levels can work together to provide safe, stable, nurturing environments for pregnant women and families with young children who are experiencing or are at risk of homelessness.

Ending Corporal Punishment in Public Schools (Key Policy Letter from the Education Secretary, December 2, 2016)[109]

On December 2, 2016, Education Secretary John B. King published a letter urging Governors and state education leaders to end corporal punishment in public schools. Corporal punishment is linked to harmful short-term and long-term outcomes for students. Below is an excerpt from Dr. King's letter.

---

[105] https://www2.ed.gov/policy/elsec/leg/essa/essaelguidance10202016.pdf

[106] https://www2.ed.gov/policy/speced/guid/idea/memosdcltrs/idea-confidentiality-requirements-faq.pdf

[107] https://www2.ed.gov/policy/gen/guid/ptac/pdf/idea-ferpa.pdf

[108] https://www.acf.hhs.gov/sites/default/files/ecd/echomelessnesspolicystatement.pdf

[109] https://www2.ed.gov/policy/elsec/guid/secletter/161122.html

"I am writing to call your attention to a practice — the use of corporal punishment — which is harmful, ineffective, and often disproportionately applied to students of color and students with disabilities. I urge you to eliminate this practice in schools."

"In-school corporal punishment entails school personnel intentionally inflicting pain on a child as punishment or to change the child's behavior. The acts of corporal punishment that are permitted when applied to children in school, if applied to adults under the laws of these states, would be prohibited as criminal assault or battery."

"School-sponsored corporal punishment is not only ineffective, it is a harmful practice, and disproportionally impacts students of color and students with disabilities. In-school corporal punishment is associated with other characteristics, like the child's race, national origin, sex, and/or disability status ...It is difficult for a school to be safe and supportive if students are afraid they will be physically punished by the adults who are charged with their learning and protecting them." Read the full text of Dr. King's letter.[110]

Juvenile Justice and Students with Disabilities

Juvenile Justice, Discipline & School Climate (Joint Guidance from Departments of Education and Justice, December 2, 2016)[111]

The Department of Education and Department of Justice (DOJ) published joint guidance to help school leaders provide transition help to youth who are reentering the community from juvenile justice facilities. The goals are to help youth as they make the transition out of juvenile justice facilities and rejoin their families, communities, continue their education, and fulfill their potential.

Publications and other resources are available at http://www.ed.gov/jjreentry

Meeting the Educational Needs of Youth Exposed to the Juvenile Justice System, Transition and Reentry Practices, 3rd ed.[112] is a transition toolkit.

Improving Outcomes for Youth with Disabilities in Juvenile Corrections[113] is a resource guide with information about evidence- and research-based practices and other resources to improve outcomes for youth with disabilities in juvenile correctional facilities.

You Got This: Educational Pathways for Youth Transitioning from Juvenile Justice Facilities[114] is a guide for incarcerated students who will reenter the community from a juvenile justice facility. The guide includes resources to give students the information they will need to continue their education after release.

Reducing Recidivism for Justice-Involved Youth[115] is a fact sheet that includes new data on correctional education from the Civil Rights Data Collection and recent enforcement efforts on correctional education issues by the Office for Civil Rights.

Preventing Racial Discrimination in Special Education

On December 12, 2016, the Department of Education and the Office for Civil Rights published **Preventing Racial Discrimination in Special Education.**[116]

---

[110] https://www2.ed.gov/policy/elsec/guid/secletter/161122.html

[111] https://www2.ed.gov/students/prep/juvenile-justice-reentry/dear-colleague-letter.pdf

[112] https://www.osepideasthatwork.org/jj/transition-and-re-entry-practices

[113] https://www.osepideasthatwork.org/jj

[114] https://www2.ed.gov/students/prep/juvenile-justice-transition/pathways-transitioning-justice-facilities.pdf

[115] https://www.ed.gov/jjreentry

[116] https://www2.ed.gov/about/offices/list/ocr/letters/colleague-201612-racedisc-special-education.pdf

During enforcement, OCR continues to find over-identification, under-identification, and unlawful delays in evaluating students of color for disabilities and whether they need special education services. OCR published this guidance to help States, school districts, and schools recognize, redress and prevent racial discrimination in special education.

Amended Regulations, Part B of the IDEA

On December 12, 2016, the Department of Education amended a few selected special education regulations under Part B of the Individuals with Disabilities Education Act (IDEA).[117] These regulations were amended to prevent racial discrimination in the identification, placement, and discipline of students with disabilities based on race or ethnicity.

The amended regulations establish a standard approach to identify disproportionate representation of students in special education, segregated settings, and disciplinary actions. Because States must use a standard methodology, it will be easier to identify disparities in disciplining students with disabilities due to race or ethnicity. The Department of Education also published this **Fact Sheet: Equity in IDEA.**[118]

Guidance on Civil Rights of Students with Disabilities

The Office for Civil Rights found that many schools do not comply with the requirements of anti-discrimination laws so they published guidance to clarify the rights of students and the responsibilities of educational institutions in several areas:

- Parent & Educator Resource Guide to Section 504 in Public Schools
- Q's and A's: Restraint and Seclusion
- Students with Disabilities Who Attend Public Charter Schools

Parent and Educator Resource Guide to Section 504 in Public Schools

The Parent and Educator Resource Guide to Section 504 in Public Schools (Office for Civil Rights, December 28, 2016)[119]

- Describes responsibilities of school districts, including obligations to provide educational services to students with disabilities.
- Outlines the steps parents can take to ensure that their children receive all the services they are entitled to receive.
- Illustrates the meaning of key terms in Section 504.
- Highlights requirements related to the identification, evaluation, and placement of students with disabilities.
- Describes procedures for handling parent-school disputes.

Wrightslaw note: This ***Parent and Educator Resource Guide to Section 504*** is an excellent resource. Pete and Pam learned many new things from it! Use it to increase your knowledge. Study it in your parent group. Make copies for educators on your child's team.

Wrightslaw note 2: To test your knowledge of Section 504, take the Wrightslaw 504 Quiz.[120]

---

[117] https://www2.ed.gov/policy/speced/reg/idea/part-b/idea-part-b-significant-disproportionality-final-regs-unofficial-copy.pdf

[118] https://www.ed.gov/news/press-releases/fact-sheet-equity-idea

[119] Download the ***Parent and Educator Guide to Section 504*** from www.wrightslaw.com/law/ocr/sec504.guide.ocr.2016.pdf

[120] http://www.wrightslaw.com/info/test.504.iq.htm

Guidance on Restraint and Seclusion

Q's & A's about Restraint and Seclusion (Office for Civil Rights, December 28, 2016)[121]

Did you know that in 2013-2014 "students with disabilities served by the IDEA represented 12% of students in public schools, but 67% of students who were subjected to restraint or seclusion in school?" The guidance is divided into four sections:

- How OCR defines restraint and seclusion
- OCR's authority to protect students with disabilities
- Legal standards OCR uses to determine whether restraint or seclusion practice violate Section 504
- Resources about the use of restraint and seclusion

Q's & A's about Restraint and Seclusion answer questions like these:

- Does Section 504 prohibit the use of restraint or seclusion in all situations?
- Can the use of restraint or seclusion deny a child from receiving FAPE?
- Where can school districts learn how to eliminate the use of restraint & seclusion in schools?

Wrightslaw note: Fact Sheet: Restraint and Seclusion of Students with Disabilities[122] - Make several copies or prints of this two-page Fact Sheet on Restraint and Seclusion to share with staff at your child's school — members of your child's team, school administrators, and school board members. **Never** assume school personnel are knowledgeable about these issues.

The U.S. Department of Education recommends that schools **never** use physical restraint or seclusion for discipline purposes, **never** use mechanical restraint, and that trained school officials use physical restraint or seclusion **only if** a child's **behavior poses imminent danger of serious physical harm** to self or others.

Wrightslaw note: The pleadings and jury instructions in *Ebonie S.*, a case about a $2.2 million-dollar jury verdict for a child who was mechanically restrained at school, are on Wrightslaw.[123]

Rights of Students with Disabilities in Public Charter Schools

This **Guidance Letter** from OSERS and OCR provides parents and the charter school community with solid information about the legal rights of charter school students with disabilities and prospective charter school students with disabilities under Section 504 and IDEA.[124]

The FAQs publications (links below) discuss how to provide equal opportunities in charter school recruitment, application, admission, enrollment and disenrollment, accessibility, nonacademic and extracurricular activities under Section 504 and IDEA.

Know Your Rights: Students with Disabilities in Charter Schools[125] a two-page summary of the rights of public charter school students with disabilities under Section 504 and IDEA.

Charter School Guidance under Section 504

FAQs about Rights of Students with Disabilities in Public Charter Schools under Section 504[126]

---

[121] https://www2.ed.gov/about/offices/list/ocr/letters/colleague-201612-504-restraint-seclusion-ps.pdf

[122] https://www2.ed.gov/about/offices/list/ocr/docs/dcl-factsheet-201612-504-restraint-seclusion-ps.pdf

[123] http://www.wrightslaw.com/law/pleadings/CO.ebonie.amended.complaint.constitutionalviolation.pdf

[124] https://www2.ed.gov/about/offices/list/ocr/letters/colleague-201612-504-charter-school.pdf

[125] https://www2.ed.gov/about/offices/list/ocr/docs/dcl-factsheet-201612-504-charter-school.pdf

[126] https://www2.ed.gov/about/offices/list/ocr/docs/dcl-faq-201612-504-charter-school.pdf

Special Education Legal Developments & Cases 2016

- Explains that charter school students with disabilities have the same rights as other public school students.
- Describes the right to nondiscrimination in recruitment, application and admission to charter schools.
- Clarifies that during the admission process, a charter school generally may not ask a prospective student if he or she has a disability.
- Reminds charter schools and parents that students with disabilities have a right to a free appropriate public education under Section 504.

Charter School Guidance under IDEA

FAQs about Rights of Students with Disabilities in Public Charter Schools under the IDEA[127]

- Emphasizes that children with disabilities who attend charter schools and their parents retain all rights and protections under IDEA, including the right to a FAPE, as they would at other public schools.
- Explains that a charter school may not unilaterally limit the services that will be provided to a student with a disability.
- Reminds charter schools about the least restrictive environment provisions that require students with disabilities to be educated with students who are not disabled, to the maximum extent appropriate.

[127] https://www2.ed.gov/policy/speced/guid/idea/memosdcltrs/faq-idea-charter-school.pdf

OSEP Letters in 2016

OSEP Letters answer questions about how to implement the ***Individuals with Disabilities Education Act (IDEA)***. OSEP Policy Letters are provided as two types of documents: OSEP Memos and Dear Colleague Letters.

The questions below about how to interpret the IDEA were submitted to OSEP from "stakeholders" - parents, administrators, evaluators, attorneys, and others and include OSEPs answers. Maybe you've wondered about these issues and will have your question answered.

IEP Team Meetings and Independent Educational Evaluations (IEEs) – Letter to Diana Savit (OSEP Policy Letter, 01/19/16)[128]

Question: "*I have concerns about my school district's policy about recording IEP Team meetings. Is a public school permitted to suspend recording an IEP meeting based upon its decision that the parent had an adequate opportunity to fully understand the meeting?*"

OSEP Response: "IDEA does not address the use of recording devices at IEP meetings . . . If the SEA has a policy that prohibits or limits recording of meetings, that policy must provide exceptions to ensure that parents understand the IEP or IEP process."[129]

Question: "*Does IDEA permit public schools to have different credentialing requirements for school psychologists than for independent psychologists who conduct IEEs? DCPS requires independent psychologists who conduct IEEs to be licensed by the Department of Health but requires their school psychologists to be licensed by the State Superintendent of Education, a less rigorous standard.*"

OSEP Response: "If an IEE is at public expense, the criteria under which the evaluation is obtained, including the location and the qualifications of the examiner, must be the same as the criteria that the district uses when it initiates an evaluation[130] . . . A school district may establish requirements that an IEE examiner hold or be eligible to hold a particular license if the district requires its own staff to hold the same license."

Membership on State Advisory Panels – Letter to John D. Copenhaver (OSEP Policy Letter, 02/09/16)

Question: "*May a parent of a child who is identified as having a disability under Section 504 serve on the State advisory panel as a parent representative?*"

OSEP Response: "Each State must have an advisory panel to provide policy guidance about special education and related services for children with disabilities in the State[131]. . . The IDEA does not prohibit a State Advisory Panel from including parents of students who have disabilities under Section 504."[132]

IEP Meeting: Parent Accompanied by an Attorney – Letter to Mr. David Andel, Illinois State Board of Education (OSEP Policy Letter, 02/17/16)[133]

Question 1: "*If a parent is accompanied to an IEP meeting by an attorney, without notifying the school in advance, is it appropriate or allowable for the school to: (1) inform the parent that the IEP meeting cannot proceed with the attorney; and/or (2) postpone the IEP meeting because the individual invited was an attorney so the meeting needs to be rescheduled to a time when the school can have legal representation?*"

---

[128] https://www2.ed.gov/policy/speced/guid/idea/memosdcltrs/savit-dcps-policies1-1-19-2016.pdf

[129] https://www2.ed.gov/policy/speced/guid/idea/memosdcltrs/letter-to-copenhaver-12-26-2016.pdf

[130] 34 CFR §300.502(e)).

[131] 34 CFR §300.167

[132] https://www2.ed.gov/policy/speced/guid/idea/memosdcltrs/16-000587-ut-copenhaver-sap.pdf

[133] https://www2.ed.gov/policy/speced/guid/idea/memosdcltrs/15-017791-il-andel-iepteam-acc.pdf

Question 2: *"Is a parent's right to invite an individual of his or her choosing hindered if the school cancels and reschedules an IEP meeting because the parent is accompanied to the meeting by an attorney without giving notice to the school?"*

OSEP Response: "IDEA does not require a parent to provide advance notice if he or she intends to invite an individual with knowledge or expertise about the child, including an attorney . . . Although IDEA does not require parents to provide advance notice, we believe parents should provide advance notice if he or she intends to bring an attorney to an IEP meeting. If postponing the meeting will not cause a delay or denial in providing a free appropriate public education to the child, the school may reschedule the meeting."

IEP Development, Review and Revision, Placement, and Hearing Decisions – Letter to Anonymous (OSEP Policy Letter, 03/03/16)[134]

Question: *"Is it permissible for New York to have a regulation that requires the board of education to approve/determine services and setting after the child's individualized education program (IEP) is developed by the Committee on Special Education?"*

OSEP Response: "Nothing in IDEA prohibits a State from having the regulation you describe, as long as the Board is not permitted to unilaterally change a child's IEP and/or placement . . . the State must ensure that the Board's actions do not delay or deny the provision of a free appropriate public education (FAPE) to the child."

Question: *"What is the timeline for developing the child's IEP after a determination of eligibility is made?"*

OSEP Response: "A meeting to develop an IEP for a child must occur within 30 days after determining that the child needs special education and related services."[135]

Question: *"Is it permissible for an SEA to redact the names of the hearing officers and district and case numbers when it makes due process findings and decisions available to the public?"*

OSEP Response: "After deleting any personally identifiable information of the child, the State (SEA) must make the findings and decisions available to the public."[136] The State should not redact the names of the hearing officers and district and case numbers unless releasing this information would result in the release of personally identifiable information."

Question: *"Is it permissible for New York to require a physician's prescription to provide a related service for a child with a disability?"*

OSEP Response: "The requirement for a physician's prescription for a related service is not inconsistent with the IDEA, provided: (1) the child's parent does not have to pay for the prescription; and (2) the requirement does not cause a delay in providing a related service that the child needs to receive FAPE."[137]

Evaluation, Eligibility, Dyslexia, Dyscalculia and Dysgraphia, Specific Learning Disabilities – Letter to Kelli Unnerstall, Decoding Dyslexia Missouri (OSEP Policy Letter, 04/25/16)[138]

Question: *"Can a school district, through their evaluation by a multi-disciplinary team including a school psychologist or a school psychological examiner, identify a child as having dyslexia under the category of Specific Learning Disability?"*

OSEP Response: "The school must ensure that the child is assessed in all areas related to the suspected disability, including as appropriate, academic performance."[139]

---

[134] https://www2.ed.gov/policy/speced/guid/idea/memosdcltrs/16-000584-iepdevelopmentandimplementation-acc.pdf

[135] 34 CFR §300.323(c)(1).

[136] 34 CFR §§300.513(d)(2) & 300.514(c)(2).

[137] https://www2.ed.gov/policy/speced/guid/idea/memosdcltrs/16-000584-iepdevelopmentandimplementation-acc.pdf

[138] https://www2.ed.gov/policy/speced/guid/idea/memosdcltrs/oseplettertounnerstall4-25-16dyslexia.pdf

"If the school determines through the evaluation process that an assessment for dyslexia is needed to ascertain whether the child has a disability and the child's educational needs, including those related to the child's reading difficulties, then the public agency must conduct the necessary assessments."

Extended Part C Option (34 CFR §303.211) – Letter to Martha Goodman, Coordinator, Maryland Special Needs Advocacy Project (OSEP Policy Letter, 05/09/16)[140]

Question: *"Is there a 'Federal barrier' to the development of an individualized education program (IEP) for an eligible child whose parent is deciding whether to choose special education and related services under Part B of the Individuals with Disabilities Education Act (IDEA or Act) or continue to receive IDEA Part C services when a State opted to make Part C early intervention services available to children aged three and older consistent with 34 CFR §303.211?"*

OSEP Response: "Each State may implement a policy under which parents of children who receive early intervention services and are eligible to receive services under Part B of the Act can continue to receive early intervention services under Part C. If a State adopts this policy, it must specify how long early intervention services will be available to these children, which could be until the beginning of the school year following the child's third, fourth, or fifth birthdays, but no later than the age when the child is eligible to enter kindergarten or elementary school."[141]

Due Process Hearings, Open or Closed – Letter to Michael J. Eig (OSEP Policy Letter, 08/04/16)[142]

Question 1: *"Are parents permitted to invite educational professionals or others not involved in their case but who are interested in learning more about due process proceedings?"*

OSEP Response: "If you are asking if the parent is permitted to invite other observers to a due process hearing that the parent does not want to open to the public, we believe the parent may invite these other individuals."[143]

Question 2: *"Can parents invite members of the press to observe the due process proceedings?"*

OSEP Response: "If parents wish to invite members of the press to observe and report on the due process hearing for their child, the hearing would be open to the public because information discussed in the proceedings would be disseminated to the public or otherwise published."

Question 3: *"Do parents have the right to open the hearing to selected individuals without opening the hearing to all the public?"*

OSEP Response: "See responses to Questions 1 and 2, which discuss the flexibility available to parents in these situations."

Question 4: *"Does the school system have a legal right to object to a parent's decision to open a due process hearing to the public?"*

OSEP Response: "The IDEA does not limit a parent's right to open a due process hearing to the public. The school does not have a legal right to contest a parent's decision to open the hearing to the public . . ."[144]

Multidisciplinary Evaluations, Eligibility, Screening Procedures Under Part C of the IDEA – Letter to Regina Skyer (OSEP Policy Letter, 08/18/16)[145]

---

[139] 34 CFR §300.304(c)(4).

[140] https://www2.ed.gov/policy/speced/guid/idea/memosdcltrs/oseplettertogoodman5-9-16.pdf

[141] 34 CFR §§303.211.

[142] https://www2.ed.gov/policy/speced/guid/idea/memosdcltrs/osep-letter-fg-8-04-16.pdf

[143] 34 CFR §300.512(c).

[144] 34 CFR §300.512(c)(2).

[145] https://www2.ed.gov/policy/speced/guid/idea/memosdcltrs/16-000770-ny-skyer-posting.pdf

Question: "*Are parents entitled to a complete multidisciplinary evaluation after they refer their child to the early intervention program?*"

OSEP Response: "The IDEA Part C regulations state that lead agencies must ensure that, subject to parental consent, each child under the age of three who is referred for evaluation or early intervention services receives a timely, comprehensive, multidisciplinary evaluation, unless eligibility is established by medical or other records."[146]

Question: "*What constitutes a multidisciplinary evaluation?*"

OSEP Response: "'Multidisciplinary' means the involvement of two or more separate disciplines or professions[147]

Question: "*Who determines a child's eligibility?*"

OSEP Response: "Qualified personnel[148] use clinical opinion and procedures to determine the child's eligibility. . . informed clinical opinion can be an independent basis for establishing eligibility, but informed clinical opinion may not be used to negate the results of evaluation instruments used to establish eligibility."[149]

Question: *"Is an early intervention official correct in telling a parent that her child will only be 'screened' to determine eligibility?"*

OSEP Response: "States have the option to adopt screening procedures[150] . . . if a child is suspected of having a disability, or if the parent requests an evaluation, an evaluation must be conducted to determine eligibility, once parental consent is obtained.[151] A parent has the right to request an evaluation even if the screening or other information indicates that the child is not suspected of having a disability."

Question: "*What constitutes a screening?*"

OSEP Response: "Screening procedures are activities carried out to identify infants and toddlers suspected of having a disability and in need of Early Intervention Services (EIS); and include appropriate [assessment] instruments by personnel trained to administer those instruments."[152]

Question: "*Is an early intervention official correct in telling a parent that her child is only entitled to be evaluated in three areas of need for the child's entire tenure under the early intervention program?*"

OSEP Response: "No. The multidisciplinary evaluation must identify the child's level of functioning in each developmental area: cognitive development; physical development, including vision and hearing; communication development; social or emotional development; and adaptive development."[153]

Due Process, RTI, General Supervision – Letter to Perry Zirkel (OSEP Policy Letter, 08/22/16)[154]

Question: "*Is an expedited due process hearing mandatory when a due process complaint is submitted pursuant to 34 CFR §300.532(a), or may a parent or local educational agency (LEA) request that a hearing pursuant to 34 CFR §300.532(a) not be subject to the expedited due process timeline? May the parties waive, via mutual agreement, the "opportunity" for an expedited hearing in a case that fits within the subject matter of 34 CFR §300.532(c)?*"

---

[146] 34 CFR §303.321(a)(1).

[147] 34 CFR §303.24.

[148] 34 CFR §303.31.

[149] 34 CFR §303.31.

[150] 34 CFR §303.320.

[151] 34 CFR §303.320(a)(3).

[152] 34 CFR §303.320(b).

[153] 34 CFR §303.21(a)(1).

[154] https://www2.ed.gov/policy/speced/guid/idea/memosdcltrs/oseplettertozirkel8-22-16.pdf

OSEP Response: "As OSEP explained in *Letter to Snyder* (December 13, 2015),[155] IDEA and its implementing regulations do not contain a provision that gives a hearing officer the authority to extend the timeline for issuing this determination at the request of a party to an expedited due process hearing.[156] IDEA Part B regulations do not permit parties to a due process complaint that involves disciplinary issues to waive the timelines."[157]

Question: "*Based on the growing body of research and experience related to Response to Intervention (RTI), does OSEP extend legal recognition to fidelity ... as an additional distinguishing and necessary core characteristic that a few States have expressly included in their RTI laws?*"

OSEP Response: "While OSEP provides guidance . . . to support SEAs and school districts in their implementation efforts, this should not be viewed as requiring the use of a particular RTI approach with specific core components or characteristics, to meet the requirement in 34 CFR §300.307(a)(2)."

Question: "*Does the IDEA regulation in 34 CFR §300.600(e), which requires SEAs to assure correction of noncompliance with free appropriate public education requirements and other specified IDEA obligations within one year, apply to corrective action orders of the complaint resolution process and to the remedies in due process hearing decisions?*"

OSEP Response: "When a State identifies noncompliance with IDEA requirements, the noncompliance must be corrected as soon as possible, and no later than one year after identification of the noncompliance."[158]

"The SEA must advise the district involved in the complaint of their findings of noncompliance and the corrective action required, and must ensure that corrective action is completed as soon as possible, and no later than one year after the noncompliance was identified."[159]

Children with Disabilities Placed in Private Schools by their Parents and Coordinated Early Intervening Services (CEIS) - Letter to Martha Goodman (OSEP Policy Letter, 08/23/16)[160]

Question: "*Can an LEA identified with significant disproportionality under Part B of the IDEA take off the top expenses related to providing comprehensive CEIS before the State or LEA calculates the proportionate share of IDEA funds that must be used by the LEA to provide special education and related services to parentally-placed private school children with disabilities?*"

OSEP Response: "No. The calculations for the comprehensive CEIS and the proportionate share must be based on the total amount of the subgrant the LEA receives . . . an LEA that is required to use Part B funds for comprehensive CEIS or voluntarily use up to the maximum amount of Part B funds for CEIS cannot adjust its local maintenance of effort (MOE) . . ."[161]

Question: "*Are States or LEAs allowed to receive Medicaid reimbursement for parentally-placed private school children with disabilities selected to receive special education or related services through services plans? If so, can that reimbursement be used to offset the proportionate share amount that the LEA must expend?*"

OSEP Response: "The proportionate amount of Part B funds that each LEA must expend on the provision of special education and related services for parentally-placed children with disabilities who attend private schools . . . is calculated based on an LEA's total sub-grant . . . other Federal funding sources may not be used to offset or reduce the . . .Part B funds that the LEA is required to expend on equitable services . . . Medicaid

---

[155] See OSEP Letter to Snyder at https://www2.ed.gov/policy/speced/guid/idea/memosdcltrs/15-012744-ca-snyder-exdueprocess-clearance.pdf

[156] https://www2.ed.gov/policy/speced/guid/idea/memosdcltrs/oseplettertozirkel8-22-16.pdf

[157] 34 CFR §300.532(c).

[158] 34 CFR §300.600(e).

[159] Question B-31 in Questions and Answers on IDEA Part B Dispute Resolution Procedures (Q&A)

[160] https://www2.ed.gov/policy/speced/guid/idea/memosdcltrs/osep-letter-to-goodman-private-school-children8-23-16.pdf

[161] 34 CFR §§300.205(d) and 300.226(a).

funds are intended to provide financial relief to school districts in meeting their responsibilities to provide FAPE to children with disabilities . . ."[162]

Parent's Right to Examine Education Records - to Nisha Kashyap, Esq., Alliance for Children's Rights (OSEP Policy Letter, 09/23/16)[163]

Question: "*Is the right to examine education records limited only to parents of children who already have been deemed eligible for special education services, or does the right extend to parents of children with suspected disabilities?"*

OSEP Response: "We believe a parent's right to inspect and review a child's education records extends to parents who suspect that their child may have a disability."

Independent Educational Evaluations – Letter to Jennifer Carroll (OSEP Policy Letter, 10/22/16)[164]

Question: "*After a district's evaluation is complete and the parent communicates a desire for their child to be assessed in an area about which they have not previously expressed concern, would the district have an opportunity to conduct an evaluation in the given area before a parent invokes the right to an IEE?"*

OSEP Response: "If the parent disagrees with the district's evaluation, the parent has a right to seek an IEE at public expense even if the district's evaluation did not assess the child in all areas related to the suspected disability... The IDEA affords a parent the right to an IEE . . . and does not condition that right on a public agency's ability to cure the defects of the evaluation it conducted prior to receiving or granting the parent's request for an IEE."

Wrightslaw note: See the November 14, 2016 Georgia IEE case *Cobb County Sch. Dist. v. DB* (in Chapter 3: Cases) where school district initiated a reverse due process hearing to avoid providing the $10,000 IEE. Cobb County lost and ultimately had to pay the parent's attorney $271,527.50.

Procedural Safeguards, Communication with Attorneys – Letter to Rochelle Marcus, M.Ed., J.D. (OSEP Policy Letter, 12/27/16)[165]

Question 1: "*Does the IDEA require a school district to correspond with a parent's attorney?"*

OSEP Response: "The IDEA and implementing regulations do not require the school to communicate with a parent's attorney, aside from specific situations like an attorney who attended an IEP meeting."

Question 2: "*Should electronic mail messages (emails) written by school staff about a student be considered an educational or public record?"*

OSEP Response: "Since this issue is addressed under the Family Educational Rights and Privacy Act (FERPA), not in the IDEA, we are referring you to the Department's Family Policy Compliance Office (FPCO). Please contact Mr. Dale King, Director, FPCO, at (202) 260-3887 or by email to Dale.King2@ed.gov"

Transportation for Parentally-Placed Private School Children, Equitable Services, Consultation with Private School Reps – Letter to Ellen Chambers (OSEP Policy Letter, 12/27/16)[166]

Question: "*Are school districts required to provide transportation to parentally-placed private school children to locations outside the LEA's geographic boundaries, including across State lines?"*

---

[162] 34 CFR §300.133.

[163] https://www2.ed.gov/policy/speced/guid/idea/memosdcltrs/lettertokashya-9-23-16.pdf

[164] https://www2.ed.gov/policy/speced/guid/idea/memosdcltrs/carroll-iee-policy.pdf

[165] https://www2.ed.gov/policy/speced/guid/idea/memosdcltrs/letter-to-marcus-12-27-2016.pdf

[166] https://www2.ed.gov/policy/speced/guid/idea/memosdcltrs/letter-to-chambers-12-27-2016.pdf

OSEP Response: "If a private school child with a disability needs transportation to benefit from or participate in the services provided under the private school provisions in IDEA, the district must provide transportation from the child's school or the child's home to a site other than the private school, and from the service site to the private school or to the child's home . . . nothing in IDEA requires school districts to provide transportation from the home of a parentally-placed private school child with a disability to the private school."[167]

"In keeping with the **best interests of the child** (emphasis added), the school district should provide services at the child's private school so the child's education is not unduly interrupted, unless there is a compelling reason for these services to be provided off-site . . . Failure to provide transportation could deny the child an opportunity to benefit from the services that the LEA determined through consultation to offer its parentally-placed private school children with disabilities."

State Advisory Panel Membership – Letter to John Copenhaver (OSEP Policy Letter, 12/27/16)[168]

Question 1: "*May the parent of a child with a disability serve on the State Advisory Panel (SAP) if he or she resides in another State?*"

OSEP Response: "The IDEA and implementing regulations do not address whether a parent must reside in the State in which they serve on an Advisory panel. The State where the child resides could appoint the parent to its Advisory Panel, even if the parent resides in another State."

Question 2: "*Would the State be responsible for paying for the parent's transportation costs if he or she served on the SAP?*"

OSEP Response: "The State educational agency (SEA) may use part of its IDEA Part B grant . . . which could include reimbursement for the travel costs of Advisory Panel members[169] . . . If the State uses teleconferencing, the State should implement measures to ensure that members who participate remotely can participate in meetings and comment on any matters before the Advisory Panel."

In Summation

In this chapter, you learned about legal news and developments from the weird, wild world of special education. If you read the articles in the **Denied** series about how unelected bureaucrats in the Texas Education Agency created a scheme to prevent children from disabilities from getting the services they need, you are likely to feel sad and angry. We share those feelings.

You have summaries of the major policy letters published by the Department of Education (ED), Office of Special Education and Rehabilitation Services (OSERS, Office of Special Education Programs (OSEP), and the Office for Civil Rights (OCR).

These resources are top-notch and can be used to educate yourself, your support group, your child's team, your school board, and/or an education reporter with the local newspaper.

In the next chapter, you'll review decisions from the Courts of Appeals - with a little help from the Table of Decisions that begins on page 44.

[167] 34 CFR §300.139(b); IDEA regulations are published in the Federal Register at http://www.wrightslaw.com/idea/law/FR.v71.n156.pdf

[168] https://www2.ed.gov/policy/speced/guid/idea/memosdcltrs/letter-to-copenhaver-12-26-2016.pdf

[169] 34 CFR §300.704.

This page intentionally left blank.

Chapter 3

Special Education Legal Decisions in 2016

Chapter 3 includes all significant decisions in special education cases by the Courts of Appeals from January 1 through December 31, 2016. The chapter begins with a Table of Decisions that lists decisions in chronological order and includes the date, circuit, author of decision if known, an abbreviated "style of the case," key issues addressed in the ruling, outcome and prevailing party. After the Table of Decisions is a comprehensive discussion of each case.

Some cases do not include the name of the Judge who authored the decision. These cases are usually identified by the Court as "Per Curiam" decisions and are delivered as rulings by the Court, acting collectively, and not by a specific judge.

Cases in which the Individuals with Disabilities Education Act (IDEA) was not an issue and roughly half a dozen "Summary" decisions by Courts of Appeal that included minimal detail and law are not included in this book.

The first book in this series, ***Wrightslaw: Special Education Legal Developments and Cases 2015*** included links to the decisions on Google Scholar. A few months after that book was published, Google changed some of these links. This led to confusion so we decided against including the Google Scholar links in this book. If you want the full text of a decision, follow the instructions for using Google Scholar in Chapter 4.

When a decision includes a reference to a statute, regulation, or to another case with the legal citation, we omitted that citation and inserted [Caselaw cite omitted]. If the reference is to a statute or regulation, we inserted [Legal cite omitted].

Cases that have an IDEA issue and a Section 504 / ADA issue usually include language like this:

> "The related statutory schemes at issue here are the Individuals with Disabilities in Education Act ('IDEA'), 20 U. S. C. §§ 1400- 1491; section 504 of the Rehabilitation Act of 1973 ('Section 504'), 29 U. S. C. § 794; and Title II of the Americans with Disabilities Act ('ADA'), 42 U. S. C. §§ 12131-12134."

If the case is an IDEA case, with no involvement of Section 504 and ADA, the decision will have references to 20 U. S. C. §§ 1400- 1491.

Footnotes in this chapter were added by the authors, not by the courts.

Fry and *Endrew F.*

In ***Wrightslaw: Special Education Legal Developments and Cases 2015,*** we provided extensive discussions of two decisions, *Fry v. Napoleon* (6th Circuit) and *Endrew F. v. Douglas Sch. Dist. RE-1* (10th Circuit). Both cases were appealed to the Supreme Court of the United States (SCOTUS) which unanimously reversed the lower court decisions.

The rulings were issued just before this book was published. Some decisions issued by Courts of Appeals in 2016 would have had different outcomes if these decisions from SCOTUS were the "law of the land."

Fry v. Napoleon Comm. Schools

In the Sixth Circuit's decision in *Fry v. Napoleon Comm. Schools,*[170] the parents did not exhaust their administrative remedies, i.e., request a special education due process hearing, to resolve their dispute. They bypassed that stage and filed suit in Federal Court. The Sixth Circuit dismissed the *Fry* case because, pursuant to 20 U. S. C. § 1415(l), the parents failed to exhaust their administrative remedies.

On February 22, 2017 SCOTUS issued a ruling on behalf of parents and reversed the Court of Appeals.[171]

SCOTUS held that a parent does not need to exhaust their administrative remedies in scenarios such as presented in *Fry*. The Court explained:[172]

> [IDEA's] §1415(l)'s exhaustion rule hinges on whether a lawsuit seeks relief for the denial of a free appropriate public education. If a lawsuit charges the FAPE was denied, the plaintiff cannot escape §1415(l) merely by bringing her suit under a statute other than the IDEA. (page 12 of decision)
>
> [However, a] complaint seeking redress for those other harms, independent of any FAPE denial, is not subject to §1415(l)'s exhaustion rule because, once again, the only "relief" the IDEA makes "available" is relief for the denial of a FAPE. (page 13 of decision)
>
> We hold that exhaustion is not necessary when the gravamen of the plaintiff's suit is something other than the denial of the IDEA's core guarantee - what the Act calls a "free appropriate public education." §1412(a)(1)(A). (page 1 of decision)

In 2016, there were conflicting rulings among federal courts about whether and when exhaustion of administrative remedies is required. As you read the cases in this book, you will see that judges dismissed cases about special education staff abusing children with disabilities because the parents failed to exhaust their administrative remedies. After the decision in *Fry*, the number of jury trials filed pursuant to Section 504 and ADA claims may increase.

Endrew F. v. Douglas Sch. Dist. RE-1

SCOTUS accepted *Endrew F.* to clarify questions about educational benefit under the Individuals with Disabilities Education Act (IDEA). Is a child with a disability under IDEA entitled to "some" educational benefit or to "meaningful" educational benefit? Courts of Appeals were split about what was required, pursuant to the 1982 decision in the *Rowley* case.[173]

In *Endrew v. Douglas Sch. Dist. RE-1,*[174] the Tenth Circuit held that the child was entitled to "some" or "de minimis" educational benefit, not to "meaningful" educational benefit.

---

[170] *Fry v. Napoleon Comm. Sch. Dist.* 788 F.3d 622 (6th Cir. 2015) is at http://www.wrightslaw.com/law/caselaw/2017/ussupct.fry.napoleon.15-497.pdf

[171] http://www.wrightslaw.com/law/caselaw/2017/ussupct.fry.napoleon.15-497.pdf

[172] 580 U.S. ___ (2017).

[173] http://www.wrightslaw.com/law/caselaw/ussupct.rowley.htm

[174] *Endrew v. Douglas Sch. Dist. RE-1,* 798 F.3d 1329 (10th Cir. 2015).

SCOTUS did not reverse its earlier decision in *Rowley* that defined the legal term "Free Appropriate Public Education" (FAPE) but made it clear that Amy Rowley was not a typical child with a disability. *Rowley* "had no need to provide concrete guidance with respect to a child who is not fully integrated in the regular classroom and not able to achieve on grade level. That case concerned a young girl who was progressing smoothly through the regular curriculum." (page 14 of decision) In 1982, "we expressly 'confine[d] our analysis' to the facts of the [*Rowley*] case before us." (page 6 of decision)

SCOTUS explained that the *Rowley* standard is applicable to children with disabilities who are fully integrated in mainstream, full inclusion settings, but does not necessarily apply to children in other settings.

In the *Endrew* decision,[175] the Court explained:

> "A focus on the particular child is at the core of the IDEA. The instruction offered must be 'specially designed' to meet a child's 'unique needs' through an '[i]ndividualized education program.' §§1401(29)(page 14 of decision). An IEP is not a form document. It is constructed only after careful consideration of the child's present levels of achievement, disability, and potential for growth. §§1414(d)(1)(A)(i)(I)–(IV), (d)(3)(A)(i)–(iv)."[176]
>
> "When all is said and done, a student offered an educational program providing 'merely more than de minimis' progress from year to year can hardly be said to have been offered an education at all. For children with disabilities, receiving instruction that aims so low would be tantamount to 'sitting idly . . . awaiting the time when they were old enough to 'drop out.'"
>
> "The IDEA demands more. It requires an educational program reasonably calculated to enable a child to make progress appropriate in light of the child's circumstances." (page 14 of decision)

You can download the decision in *Endrew F.*[177] and a discussion of the case from Wrightslaw.[178] *Endrew F.* is likely to have a substantial positive impact on judges as they assess the expected level of progress and educational benefit that children receive from their IEPs.[179]

A Note about Later Outcomes and Attorneys

In some of the cases in this chapter, we learned about new developments after the decision was issued. This came about in part because we are members of the Council of Parent Attorneys and Advocates (COPAA).[180]

COPAA is an organization whose members are special education attorneys, lay advocates, related service providers, parents of children with special education needs, and others who are interested in special education law. The authors are charter members of COPAA and helped to establish the organization during the 1990's.

COPAA filed amicus briefs on behalf of children with disabilities and their parents in several Court of Appeals cases in this book.

Some decisions provided the names of the attorneys who were counsel so we included their names with our discussion on the case.

---

[175] 580 U.S. ___ (2017).

[176] The complete IEP statute, 20 U.S.C. § 1414(d), begins on page 99 in ***Wrightslaw: Special Education Law, 2nd Ed.***

[177] http://www.wrightslaw.com/law/caselaw/2017/ussupct.endrew.douglas.15-827.pdf

[178] http://www.wrightslaw.com/law/art/endrew.douglas.scotus.analysis.htm

[179] On March 27, 2017, in *M.C. v. Antelope Valley Union High School District*, (Case # 14-56344) the Ninth Circuit reversed decisions by an Administrative Law Judge and U.S. District Court based on the new heightened *Endrew* standard.

[180] http://www.copaa.org/

This page intentionally left blank.

Table 1. Table of Decisions in Special Education Cases in 2016

Date	Circuit Judge State	Short Style F.3d Cite, if any	Description
1/5/2016	9th Cir. CA	*AR v. Santa Monica Malibu Sch. Dist*	Tuition reimbursement, private placement case with least restrictive environment (LRE) issue. Discussion of the *Rachel Holland* case.
1/8/2016	3rd Cir. Scirica PA	*Norristown Sch. Dist. v. FC*	Tuition reimbursement / attorney fee case. Child was moved from self-contained placement to more general ed; behavior regressed. Parent made unilateral placement.
1/13/2016	5th Cir. Higginbotham LA	*Seth B v. Orleans Parish Sch. Bd* 810 F. 3d 961	Independent Educational Evaluation was alleged to be noncompliant with State IEE standards and the $8,000 cost exceeded the State's $3,000 cap. School board refused to pay any amount.
1/20/2016	2nd Cir. Lohier NY	*TK v. NYC DOE* 810 F.3d 869	School's refusal to address parent's concerns about bullying at an IEP meeting was a violation of procedural safeguards that resulted in denial of FAPE and entitlement to tuition reimbursement, advance deposit notwithstanding.
2/2/2016	5th Cir. TX	*Crawford v. San Marcos Sch. Dist*	Third lawsuit dismissed pursuant to "res judicata" because parent "could have and should have raised her ADA claims in her first lawsuit against the District." She failed to pursue ADA claim at same time she pursued IDEA claim.
2/3/2016	2nd Cir. NY	*Frank v. Sachem Sch. Dist. and NY SEA*	Placement, LRE. After child placed in more restrictive placement, parent sued under ADA alleging a violation of *Olmstead's* "integration mandate." Custodial parent consented to the placement. Lower court dismissed because alleged misconduct was neither intentional nor based on deliberate indifference.
2/5/2016	6th Cir. Kethledge KY	*RK v. Scott County Bd. of Ed*	Placement, discrimination, damages. School did not allow child with diabetes to attend his neighborhood school for KG and 1st grade; allowed him to attend in 2nd grade. Parents sued, alleged violations of ADA and Section 504, sought dollar damages.
2/16/2016	OK Sup. Ct. Watt OK	*Oliver v. Hofmeister*	State taxpayers filed a declaratory judgment action, seeking to enjoin tuition payment to private sectarian schools; alleged that state Scholarships for Students with Disabilities Act violated State Constitution. Since funds were paid to parents who decided on school child would attend, program did not violate State Constitution.

Special Education Legal Developments & Cases 2016

2/19/2016	10th Cir. Matheson NM	*JV v. Albuquerque Pub. Sch.* 813 F.3d 1289 (10th Cir. 2016)	During a behavioral outburst, child with autism was handcuffed. Parent filed suit alleging violation of ADA.
2/22/2016	9th Cir. CA	*Anaheim Union High Sch. Dist. v. JE*	Attorney's fee case. After prevailing on the merits, parent appealed the reduction of attorney fee hourly rate to $400/hour and denial of paralegal costs. Court held that $400/hour was in line with prevailing rate; expert witness fees cannot be characterized as paralegal fees.
2/23/2016	5th Cir. Prado LA	*Tina M. v. St. Tammany Parish Sch. Bd* 816 F.3d 57 (5th Cir. 2016)	Attorneys' fees are not available unless there is a favorable decision on the merits. A stay-put order is an injunction that is automatic and is not related to the merits of the case.
3/3/2016	9th Cir. LeMelle AZ	*AG v. Paradise Valley Unif Such Dist.* 815 F.3d 1195 (9th Cir. 2016)	**2016 Case of the Year** Case involved failure re FBA and BIP and change of placement. FAPE under IDEA is different from FAPE under 504 / ADA. Parental consent to IEP for FAPE under IDEA may not be sufficient for FAPE under 504 / ADA. Required reading for all spec ed attorneys.
3/4/2016	2nd Cir. NY	*LK v. Sewanhaka Cent High Sch. Dist.*	Parents failed to exhaust their administrative remedies. Case is similar to the *Fry* case decided by SCOTUS.
3/9/2016	5th Cir. Higginson TX	*Cripps v. Hurst-Euless-Bedford Indep. Sch. Dist.*	Discipline case. Manifestation Determination Review (MDR) concluded that child's misconduct was not related to ADHD; school did not retaliate against the child because of child's disability.
3/10/2016	5th Cir. Dennis TX	*Rockwall Indep. Sch. Dist. v. MC* 816 F.3d 329	Tuition reimbursement case. Even if public school program is not appropriate, reimbursement can be denied because of parent unreasonableness regarding the IEP process.
3/16/2016	2nd Cir. NY	*JC v. NYC DOE*	Tuition reimbursement case. Pursuant to the *Burlington - Carter* test, failure to implement FBA / BIP does not render an IEP legally inadequate if the IEP adequately identifies the student's behavioral impediments and implements strategies to address that behavior.
3/21/2016	3rd Cir. McKee PA	*EC v. Philadelphia Sch. Dist*	Philadelphia sought to reduce attorney fee award to prevailing parents because of city's "distressed" financial condition.
3/22/2016	DC Cir. Tatel DC	*BD v. DCPS* 817 F. 3d 792	Court of Appeals provides a comprehensive discussion about how to determine an appropriate award of compensatory education. Court reversed the award of limited comp ed, required more and addressed enforcement of a special education due process ruling.

3/24/2016	11th Cir. GA	*SM v. Gwinnett County Sch. Dist*	LRE mainstreaming case. Upheld school's IEP that provided regular ed all day except for "direct, explicit, small group instruction with drill and repetition" in "reading, writing and math."
4/5/2016	5th Cir. Costa TX	*Rideau v. Keller Indep. Sch. Dist* 819 F. 3d 155	Teacher abuse, damages case. Special ed teacher physically abused a student. Jury awarded one million dollars. After trial, school learned that incompetent child (now adult) had a trust. School asserted that parents did not have standing to sue. District Court struck verdict. Appealed to Fifth Circuit.
4/8/2016	4th Cir. Harris MD	*SB v. Harford County Bd. of Ed* 819 F. 3d 69	Bullying case. Court held that evidence was insufficient to find that bullying was based on child's disability, thus not a 504 violation.
4/13/2016	10th Cir. Baldock NM	*R.M-G. v. Bd. of Ed. Las Vegas NM*	Attorneys fee case. Full award of attorney fees upheld by Circuit Court; upheld "fees on fees" award and remanded back for fee calculation for Circuit Court appeal.
5/2/2016	4th Cir. MD	*Se.H. v. Anne Arundel Bd. of Ed*	Child has cerebral palsy, severe food allergies, asthma, a swallowing disorder, seizure disorder, feeding difficulties and vision problems. Parents wanted IEP to provide an individual trained in Heimlich and CPR by child's side at all times.
5/4/2016	2nd Cir. NY	*JS v. NYC DOE*	Appeal of tuition reimbursement case. Rulings by Hearing Officer, Review Officer and District Court that public school provided FAPE upheld.
5/6/2016	2nd Cir. NY	*HB v. Byram Hills Cent Sch. Dist*	Exhaustion case. Hearing Officer became ill which led to significant delays while waiting for a decision. Parents filed suit in federal court; case dismissed because they failed to exhaust administrative remedies.
5/10/2016	10th Cir. Murphy UT	*MS v. Utah Sch. for Deaf and Blind* 822 F. 3d 1128	Compensatory education and determination of subsequent placement. District Court left remedy for comp ed and placement to the IEP team that previously failed to provide child with FAPE.
5/13/2016	9th Cir. CA	*Douglas v. CA OAH v. JC + Cupertino Sch. Dist*	Unusual case between two state departments, the OAH, two school districts, and parents about statutory interpretation regarding OT services and dispute resolution authority.
5/20/2016	2nd Cir. Wesley NY	*LO v. NYC DOE* 822 F. 3d 95	**2016 Case of the Year** Like *AG v. Paradise Valley*, this is a major decision. Issues include 3 years of procedural violations, BIPs and FBAs. Parents lost at due process, at review, in District Court. Second Circuit reversed. Student was 20 years old, equitable relief ordered to extend beyond 22nd birthday.

Special Education Legal Developments & Cases 2016

5/20/2016	9th Cir. Bea CA	*Smith + Munoz v. Los Angeles Unif. Sch. Dist* 822 F.3d 1065	California's *Chandra Smit*h Decree to increase LRE resulted in special ed centers closing. Parents wanted to intervene but District Court denied.
5/23/2016	9th Cir. Reinhardt CA	*Timothy O v. Paso Robles Unif. Sch. Dist* 822 F.3d 1105	**2016 Case of the Year** Case about legal requirements to determine if a child has autism. Child was found not eligible based on opinion of school psychologist but psychologist did not evaluate. Early intervention and diagnosis needed, not provided, child damaged.
6/10/2016	6th Cir. Cole OH	*WR v. Ohio Dept. Health*	ABA services for child with autism, failure to exhaust. under Part C of IDEA. parent sued Dept. of Health for failure to provide ABA services to child with autism. Did not request a due process hearing. Citing *Fry*, the District Court dismissed for failure to exhaust. Appealed.
6/13/2016	11th Cir. FL	*AL v. Jackson County Sch. Bd*	School district sued for sanctions against parent and attorney after parent's motion for an injunction against district dismissed. Sanctions granted. Appealed to Eleventh Circuit; vacated finding that the motion was frivolous.
6/16/2016	6th Cir. Daughtrey MI	*Binno v. Amer. Bar Assoc.* 826 F.3d 338	Visually impaired adult alleged that poor performance on LSAT was because it required visual diagramming which he could not do. Sued ABA which did not control content or format of LSAT. Law School Admission Council was proper party but was not included by Plaintiff in suit. No standing to sue ABA.
6/16/2016	10th Cir. McHugh CO	*Ramona Smith v. Cheyenne Mountain Sch. Dist. 12*	Stay put determined to be the last school listed on IEP as the child's school of attendance, although the child no longer attended that school. Appealed to Tenth Circuit.
6/22/2016	9th Cir. Smith CA	*Baquerizo v. Garden Grove Unif. Sch. Dist.* 826 F.3d 1179	Parents sought tuition reimbursement based on June 2009 and June 2011 IEPs. Did not initiate litigation until two years after IEP meeting. Many hearings and contentious history. Court of Appeals affirmed decisions of ALJ and District Court that IEPs were appropriate. Tuition reimbursement denied.
7/7/2016	8th Cir. Riley MO	*Moore v. Kansas City Pub. Sch* 828 F. 3d 687	Child with IEP was raped in school. Lawsuit against district filed in state court. School district removed case to federal court, asserting a "Federal Question," then claimed that parents failed to "exhaust" administrative remedies. District Court agreed, dismissed case. Appeal to Eighth Circuit. Reversed and remanded case to state court.
7/14/2016	2nd Cir. NY	*Spring v. Allegany-Limestone Cent. Sch. Dist*	Special education student committed suicide because of "unrelenting harassment and bullying." Parents sued school on numerous legal theories of liability. District Court dismissed on all counts. Court of Appeals upheld reversal on

			all but one count, noting that parents should have been permitted to amend their ADA and Section 504 claims.
7/15/2016	1st Cir. Lipez ME	*Ms. S. v. Regional Sch. Unit 72* 829 F.3d 95	Tuition reimbursement and statute of limitations case. First Circuit held that the parents not entitled to last two years of tuition reimbursement, remanded case for two prior years due to concerns about the development of statute of limitations regulation.
7/15/2016	6th Cir. Boggs OH	*Gibson v. Forest Hills Sch. Dist.*	District Court held that school district violated IDEA's transition requirements to include adult child in IEP meeting; did not provide FAPE; found that attorney's fee request of $800,313 approximated "lodestar value" but only awarded $327,641 for attorney's fees. Appealed. Sixth Circuit held that school did not provide FAPE, remanded case to recalculate attorney fees.
7/25/2016	10th Cir. Holmes (Gorsuch) NM	*AM v. Holmes* 830 F.3d 1123	Child arrested and handcuffed at school for burping. Parent sued for violation of civil rights. District Court dismissed. Parent appealed to Tenth Circuit. Judge Gorsuch, newest Justice on Supreme Court, wrote a strong, pro-child, anti-school dissent.
7/26/2016	2nd Cir. NY	*MM v. NYC DOE*	Tuition reimbursement case that alleged procedural defects. District Court dismissed case. On appeal, Second Circuit upheld dismissal, noting that procedural violations result in denial of a FAPE only if they impede the child's right to FAPE . . . or cause deprivation of educational benefits.
8/5/2016	1st Cir. Lipez ME	*Doe v. Cape Elizabeth Sch. Dist.* 832 F.3d 69	Eligibility case. Can child with a strong academic record have a learning disability and need special education and related services? District Court ruled against child. First Circuit reversed and remanded back to District Court because "the district court did not make an independent judgment as to Jane's reading fluency deficit."
8/18/2016	3rd Cir. Greenaway NJ	*SD v. Haddon Heights Bd. of Ed.* 833 F. 3d 389	Another *Fry* exhaustion case which upheld dismissal because the parents failed to exhaust the administrative process for a retaliation claim. Case is on appeal to SCOTUS.
8/31/2016	3rd Cir. Rendell PA	*Swanger v. Warrior Run Sch. Dist.*	A "mentally challenged girl" placed in class with a known sexual predator who molested her. In lawsuit against district, District Court refused to allow plaintiff to review predator's confidential mental health files. On appeal, Third Circuit reversed, noting that District Court may have wrongfully deprived the parents of a chance to prove their case.

9/1/2016	9th Cir. Schroeder CA	*LJ v. Pittsburg Unif Sch. Dist.* 835 F.3d 1168 (9th Cir. 2016)	Eligibility case. District Court held that child was disabled under 3 IDEA categories [but] an IEP "was not necessary" because child's performance in general ed classes was satisfactory. Discounted role of child's suicide attempts because they happened outside of school. Appealed to 9th Circuit.
9/8/2016	6th Cir. Sutton MI	*Gohl v. Livonia Sch. Dist.* *836 F. 3d 672*	Teacher abuse case. District Court dismissed teacher's abuse of a child because not "enough evidence for a reasonable jury to find that . . . challenged actions occurred 'because of' or 'solely by reason of' J.G.'s disability." Strong dissent, noting that teacher abused child because she reported having "a 'sick sense of humor' and liked 'to target lower functioning students.'"
9/12/2016	2nd Cir. Hall NY	*Montesa v. Schwartz + East Ramapo*	Hundreds of parents sued district, alleging violation of Establishment Clause because IDEA funds diverted to private Hasidic/ Jewish schools. Parents claimed most school board members were Hasidic Jews. Board claimed immunity, parents did not have standing to sue. District Court ruled in parents' favor. On appeal, two members of Second Circuit panel agreed that parents did not have standing, dismissed case. Strong dissent filed.
9/16/2016	2nd Cir. Livingston NY	*BC v. Mt Vernon Sch. Dist.* 837 F.3d 152	Case about discrimination and failure to exhaust administrative remedies. Parents claimed that non-credit academic intervention services ('AIS') provided during school interfered with children's ability to meet credit requirements. violating IDEA, ADA, Section 504. District Court dismissed ADA/504 claims; held that parents failed to exhaust so dismissed IDEA claims.[181] Appealed to 2nd Circuit.
10/4/2016	1st Cir. ME	*Pollack v. Regional Sch. Unit 75*	Child's disabilities affect ability to communicate. After incident at school, parents sought consent for child to wear audio recording device. When school denied request, Section 504 and ADA litigation followed.
10/6/2016	2nd Cir. CT	*Dervishi v. Stamford Bd. Ed. + CT DOE*	Parent filed a 'pro se' Complaint against school district and state DOE; did not request a due process hearing. Parents' failure to exhaust administrative remedies was fatal to their case.

[181] See SCOTUS *Fry*.

11/3/2016	9th Cir. CA	*NG v. ABC Unif. Sch. Dist.*	A student was hospitalized and received special ed services from the district where hospital was located. Residential treatment was recommended after discharge. Parent asked district that provided temporary services provide this placement. District refused, claiming that after discharge, district where parent or guardian resides is responsible for IEP and placement. Parent appealed.
11/14/2016	11th Cir. GA	*Cobb County Sch. Dist. v. DB*	**2016 Case of the Year** Reverse due process, Independent Educational Evaluation (IEE), attorney fee case. School requested due process rather than provide IEE but had to pay $271,527.50+ to parents' attorney because district unreasonably protracted the litigation.
11/17/2016	9th Cir. Graber WA	*NE v. Seattle Sch. Dist.* 842 F.3d 1093	Stay-Put / Pendency case. At IEP meeting before summer break, parents agreed to continue same placement for rest of year. School proposed to change placement to self-contained for next year. Parents agreed to services, did not agree to change of placement. Parents moved to different district, did not request due process hearing. When new district placed child in self-contained class, the parents objected. Split decision: two judges held that self-contained was the current educational placement, one judge wrote a strong dissent.
11/23/2016	5th Cir. Jones TX	*Campbell v. Lamar Inst. of Tech. (LIT)*	Higher education 504 / ADA case. Student with LD received extended time, a laptop and a recorder. Wanted more accommodations, filed suit. District Court dismissed. Fifth Circuit upheld dismissal but corrected District Court's understanding of law of immunity, Section 504 and ADA. ADA's language tracks Section 504; 'remedies, procedures and rights' of Rehabilitation Act are obtainable under the ADA.
12/5/2016	5th Cir. TX	*Powers v. Northside Indep. Sch. Dist.*	"Whistleblower / Qui Tam" immunity case. Principal and asset principal terminated after they contacted state DOE to allege misconduct by administration in denying Section 504 eligibility for some students. School district claimed immunity. District Court denied immunity; Fifth Circuit upheld immunity. "When a public employee alleges a violation of the [Whistleblower] Act, the employing state or local governmental entity's immunity from suit is waived."
12/5/2016	9th Cir. OR	*Forest Grove Sch. Dist. v. Student*	"Deference" case. After parent prevailed on several issues, ALJ ordered broad range of remedial relief. District appealed to the District Court. District Court found fault with the factual and legal analysis of the ALJ and reversed. Parent appealed to the Ninth Circuit which also found substantial fault with the ALJ's analysis.

12/8/2016	9th Cir. CA	*Emma C v. Eastin + CA DOE*	In this 1996 "Consent Decree," the Court Monitor asserted that CA DOE did not provide Monitor with information needed to determine if CA DOE is complying with the Consent Decree. District Court ordered CA DOE to provide the Monitor with information needed to fulfill duties. CA DOE appealed to Ninth Circuit.
12/9/2016	DC Cir. Edwards DC	*Reed v. DCPS* 843 F. 3d 517	Attorney's fee case. District Court excluded some hours spent in settlement conferences from the fee award. Court of Appeals reversed and remanded; declined to use the *Laffey* Matrix but may have opened that door for future cases.

End of Table of Decisions

Table 2. Table of Decisions in Alphabetical Order

AG v. Paradise Valley Unif Sch Dist.	*MM v. NYC DOE*
AL v. Jackson Co Sch Bd	*Montesa v. Schwartz + East Ramapo*
AM v. Holmes	*Moore v. Kansas City Pub Sch*
Anaheim Union High Sch Dist v. JE	*MS v. Utah Sch. for Deaf and Blind*
AR v. Santa Monica Malibu Sch Dist	*MS.s v. Regional Sch. Unit 72*
Baquerizo v. Garden Grove Unif Sch Dist	*NE v. Seattle Sch Dist*
BC v. Mt Vernon Sch Dist	*NG v. ABC Unif Sch Dist*
BD v. DCPS	*Norristown Sch Dist v. FC*
Binno v. Amer Bar Assoc	*Oliver v. Hofmeister*
Campbell v. Lamar Inst. of Tech. (LIT)	*Pollack v. Regional Sch Unit 75*
Cobb County Sch Dist v. DB	*Powers v. Northside Indep Sch Dist*
Crawford v. San Marcos Sch Dist	*R.M-G. v. Bd Ed Las Vegas NM*
Cripps v. Hurst-Euless-Bedford Indep Sch Dist	*Ramona Smith v. Cheyenne Mountain Sch Dist 12*
Dervishi v. Stamford Bd Ed + CT DOE	*Reed v. DCPS*
Doe v. Cape Elizabeth Sch. District	*Rideau v. Keller Indep Sch Dist.*
Douglas v. CA OAH v. JC + Cupertino Sch Dist	*RK v. Scott County Bd of Ed*
EC v. Philadelphia Sch Dist	*Rockwall Indep. Sch Dist v. MC*
Emma C v. Eastin + CA DOE	*SB v. Harford Co Bd of Ed*
Forest Grove Sch Dist v. Student	*SD v. Haddon Heights Bd of Ed*
Frank v. Sachem Sch Dist and NY SEA	*Se.H. v. Anne Arundel Bd of Ed*
Gibson v. Forest Hills Sch Dist	*Seth B v. Orleans Parish Sch. Bd*
Gohl v. Livonia Sch Dist	*SM v. Gwinnett Co Sch Dis.*
HB v. Byram Hills Cent Sch Dist	*Smith + Munoz v. Los Angeles Unif. Sch. Dist*
JC v. NYC DOE	*Spring v. Allegany-Limestone Cent Sch Dist*
JS v. NYC DOE	*Swanger v. Warrior Run Sch Dist*
JV v. Albuquerque Pub Sch	*Timothy O v. Paso Robles Unif. Sch Dist*
LJ v. Pittsburg Unif Sch Dist.	*Tina M v. St. Tammany Parish Sch Bd*
LK v. Sewanhaka Cent High Sch. Dist.	*TK v. NYC DOE*
LO v. NYC DOE	*WR v. Ohio Dept Health*

Summaries of Cases

AR v. Santa Monica Sch. Dist.

9th Cir. 2016

California - 1/5/2016

Parents appealed a tuition reimbursement denial for a private placement. The Court of Appeals upheld the decision of the ALJ and District Court: "The School District must offer the Student a placement that is tailored to the Student's unique needs. [Caselaw cite omitted.] Additionally, the placement must be in the least restrictive environment - [LRE] in other words, the Student must be placed with non-disabled peers "to the maximum extent appropriate." [Legal cite omitted.]

"This court weighs four factors to determine whether a placement is in the least restrictive environment: (1) the educational benefits to the student if placed in general education; (2) the non-academic benefits to the student if placed in general education; (3) the effect on the teacher and classmates if the student is placed in general education; and (4) costs. *Sacramento City Uni. Sch. Dist. v. Rachel Holland*, 14 F.3d 1398 (9th Cir. 1994)

[Caselaw cite omitted.] "The School District found that the Student would not benefit from a general education placement, due to the severe symptoms of his autism."

"Although the School District provided a free appropriate public education, both substantively and procedurally, the Student's parents unilaterally placed the Student in private school. After the Student's unilateral placement, the School District was not required to provide previously consented-to services. [Legal cite omitted.] The Student's parents are also not entitled to reimbursement for the Student's private education." [Legal cite omitted.]

Outcome: School district prevailed.

Norristown Sch Dist. v. FC

3rd Cir. 2016

Pennsylvania - 1/8/2016

This issues in this case involve tuition reimbursement, unilateral placement, and attorneys' fees.

"The Norristown Area School District (school district) appeals an order from the United States District Court for the Eastern District of Pennsylvania awarding compensatory education to a student, F.C., and his parents for failing to provide F.C. with a free and appropriate public education (FAPE) for his second—and third-grade school years under the Individuals with Disabilities Education Act. [Legal cite omitted.] The school district also appeals the award of attorneys' fees and costs under IDEA's fee-shifting provision. [Legal cite omitted.] These cases have been consolidated on appeal. We will affirm."

"Initially, F.C.'s second-grade IEP recommended he continue attending the autistic-support classroom for most subjects. But in June 2011, F.C.'s IEP team changed his second-grade IEP dramatically. Under the revised IEP, F.C. would receive all his academic subjects in the general second-grade classroom without one-on-one paraprofessional support, except for writing instruction, which he would receive in a learning-support classroom. This meant that 87 percent of his total school day would be in the general classroom without one-on-one support. This IEP was implemented at the start of F.C.'s second-grade year."

"Early into second grade, F.C.'s behavior started to regress. F.C. had trouble staying on task and his classroom interruptions began to impede his learning and that of other students."

"In April 2012, a new IEP was issued for F.C.'s third-grade school year (2011-12). There was no PBSP [Positive Behavioral Support Plan] in this IEP. . . The school district revised F.C.'s third-grade IEP in June 2012 to add a PBSP, but the anticipated duration of F.C.'s para-professional support remained November 2012."

"The parents refused to sign this IEP, viewing it as inadequate, and enrolled F.C. in the Stratford

Friends School for the start of third grade. Stratford Friends is a small private school that educates students with language-based learning difficulties. F.C.'s third-grade class had eleven children and two teachers and F.C. received significant individualized attention."

"The school district also contends the court erred in holding that the school district failed to offer F.C. a FAPE for his third-grade year. We disagree. The June 2012 IEP, which was to be implemented during F.C.'s third-grade year, included one-on-one paraprofessional support, but its anticipated duration, November 2012, was five months earlier than that of every other modification."

"The school district contends that because the duration was anticipated and not actual, the parents could not preemptively remove F.C. from the school district and seek tuition reimbursement. But the adequacy of an IEP 'can only be determined as of the time it is offered to the student, and not at some later date.' [Caselaw cite omitted.] "Because one-on-one support was critical to F.C.'s ability to attain a "meaningful educational benefit," the parents were justified in questioning the adequacy of F.C.'s third-grade IEP and in removing him from the school district for third grade."

The parents were partially successful on their claims, but their claims arose from the same core of facts, and they succeeded on two issues—whether the school district failed to provide F.C. with a FAPE for second grade and third grade... [T]the court did not abuse its discretion by awarding the parents $139,629.34 for reasonable attorneys' fees and costs.

(Parent's attorney - Michael Gehring)

Outcome: Parents prevailed.

Seth B v. Orleans Parish Sch. Bd.

810 F. 3d 961 (5th Cir. 2016)

Louisiana - 1/13/2016

In this Louisiana dispute about the cost of an Independent Educational Evaluation [IEE] of a child with autism, the Court of Appeals addressed the State requirements for a $3,000 cap versus the actual cost of the evaluation.

"Seth's parents sent the Orleans Parish School Board (OPSB) a request for an IEE. The board granted the request, offering reimbursement up to $3,000 on condition that the IEE comply with Louisiana Bulletin 1508 [which] contains the state-mandated evaluation criteria . . ."

"In April 2012, they sent OPSB Dr. Brockman's report. OPSB responded the next month with a letter outlining 31 ways in which the IEE allegedly did not meet Bulletin 1508 criteria. The board invited Seth's parents to have Dr. Brockman contact them to discuss the alleged areas of noncompliance. The parents did not reply to this letter, and there is no indication that Dr. Brockman ever contacted the board."

". . . Seth's parents sent the board invoices from the IEE totaling $8,066.50 and requested reimbursement. The board . . . denied the request in a letter to Seth's parents, noting that it could not reimburse them for a noncompliant evaluation and that some of the invoices appeared unrelated to the completion of the IEE."

"Seth and his parents requested an administrative due process hearing. An ALJ . . . ruled against Seth and his parents, finding that their counsel had stipulated to the IEE's noncompliance with Bulletin 1508 and that he therefore lacked jurisdiction to award reimbursement."

"Seth and his parents sought review in federal district court . . . [which] granted summary judgment for OPSB. The court found that the board had not waived its right to challenge Seth's IEE, that the IEE did not comply with Bulletin 1508, and that reimbursement was therefore disallowed."

"The Council of Parent Attorneys and Advocates, Inc., the National Disability Rights Network, the National Federation of the Blind, and the National Association of the Deaf filed amicus briefs urging reversal. The National School Boards Association, the National Association of State Directors of Special Education, and school board associations from Louisiana, Mississippi, and Texas filed an amicus brief urging affirmance."

"Seth's IEE will 'meet agency criteria' and merit reimbursement if it substantially complies with Bulletin 1508. As noted above, the district court did not squarely address this factually specific question. We therefore remand for analysis under a substantial compliance standard. If the court below (or, upon further remand, the administrative hearing officer) finds the IEE substantially compliant, it should award reimbursement."

"In any event, however, appellants will not be entitled to the full cost of the evaluation they obtained. Appellants knew of OPSB's $3,000 cost cap for IEEs, yet they spent over $8,000. The Department of Education has explained that IDEA allows schools to enforce reasonable cost criteria for IEEs if parents in unique circumstances have the opportunity to request exemption. Here, OPSB offered appellants an opportunity to demonstrate unique circumstances in its correspondence with them over the cost cap, but appellants did not respond. Therefore, the $3,000 cap binds them."

The District Court decision was reversed and case remanded back, but the District Court has to address Bulletin 1508. Subject to that analysis, the parents may recover $3,000, but not more.

COPAA filed an Amicus brief with the Court in this case.

Outcome: Parents prevailed, partially.

TK v. NYC DOE

810 F.3d 869 (2nd Cir. 2016)

New York - 1/20/2016

The Second Circuit found that bullying can result in a denial of FAPE that justifies an award of tuition reimbursement for a private placement. . . The Court did not fault the parents for "making a precautionary private school deposit . . . in the event that their concerns about bullying remained unaddressed."

The Court explained that: "On appeal we consider whether the Department violated the IDEA by denying Plaintiffs' requests to discuss L.K.'s bullying despite their reasonable concern that the bullying interfered with L.K.'s ability to receive a free appropriate public education, also known as a 'FAPE.' We conclude that the Department's refusal to discuss the bullying of L.K. with her parents during the process of developing L.K.'s 'individualized education program,' or 'IEP,' violated the IDEA. Because Plaintiffs have also met their burden to show that their choice of a private placement for L.K. was appropriate and that the equities favored reimbursing them, we affirm the judgment of the District Court."

"Academically, L.K. made 'progress throughout the school year' and performed at or approaching grade level in all subjects. But at a certain point L.K.'s schoolmates bullied her so severely that she came home crying and complained to her parents about the bullying on a near daily basis. L.K.'s three SEITs [Special Education Itinerant Teacher] testified that her classmates constantly bullied her. One SEIT even described the classroom as a 'hostile environment' for L.K."

"A neurodevelopmental pediatrician found that the 'minimal interactions' L.K. had with her classmates 'were mostly negative.' The witnesses supported these generalized assessments by describing specific instances of bullying . . . L.K.'s teachers appear to have done little to stop the bullying."

"Even when an IEP itself is not deficient, parents may seek reimbursement for a unilateral placement if the State fails to afford them certain procedural safeguards. Of particular importance here, the IDEA requires States to provide parents with the 'opportunity to participate in the decision-making process regarding the provision of a [FAPE] to the parents' child.'" [Legal cite omitted.]

"We conclude that the Department denied L.K. a FAPE by violating her parents' procedural right to participate in the development of her IEP. At two separate meetings, both of which were integral to the development of L.K.'s IEP, Plaintiffs sought to discuss L.K.'s bullying, but school officials refused to do so."

"Nor are we persuaded that Plaintiffs engaged in any form of misconduct merely by making a precautionary private school deposit prior to the meeting with public school officials during which the IEP was developed. Summit required Plaintiffs to put down a deposit long before that meeting, and waiting would have imperiled their ability to secure a spot for L.K in the event that their concerns about bullying remained unaddressed."

(Parent's attorney - Gary S. Mayerson // School's attorney - Ronald E. Sternberg)

Outcome: Parents prevailed.

Crawford v. San Marcos Sch. Dist
5th Cir. 2016
Texas - 2/2/2016

Crawford sued the school district three times. "Her first suit against the District raised a claim pursuant to the Individuals with Disabilities Education Act ('IDEA'). Because all the events giving rise to Crawford's ADA claims had already occurred by the time Crawford filed the first suit, she could have raised her ADA claims at the same time as her IDEA claim. However, she did not do so. Crawford ultimately settled her IDEA claim against the District, and the court entered a final judgment dismissing the first case with prejudice."

The Magistrate Judge concluded "that Crawford could have and should have raised her ADA claims in her first lawsuit against the District." Her case was dismissed because the legal principle known as claim preclusion, "also known as res judicata, bars the litigation of claims that either have been litigated or should have been raised in an earlier suit."

"Crawford argues that the first case and the current case do not involve the same claim or cause of action because the IDEA claim she raised in the first case is governed by different elements than the ADA claim she raises in the instant case."

"Crawford's argument confuses two distinct doctrines with different elements. The standard Crawford cites from *Pace* applies to the doctrine of issue preclusion (also known as collateral estoppel), not claim preclusion. The two doctrines are "very different." Claim preclusion "foreclose[as] any litigation of matters that have never been litigated" because "they should have been advanced in an earlier suit."

The Court of Appeals upheld the ruling that she should have litigated her ADA claim at the same time she litigated her IDEA claim.

Outcome: School district prevailed.

Frank v. Sachem Sch. Dist. and NY SEA
2nd Cir. 2016
New York - 2/3/2016

The District Court dismissed MF's "claim for damages under the Americans with Disabilities Act principally for failure to state a claim. On appeal, Frank argues that defendant Sachem School District ('Sachem') violated MF's rights under the ADA's 'integration mandate' - which is designed to ensure that disabled individuals are provided public services in the 'most integrated setting appropriate to the [individual's] needs,' 28 C.F.R. § 35.130(d) - when it allegedly unnecessarily removed MF from public school and placed him in the Little Flower Residential Treatment Center, a center for emotionally disturbed children. Cf. *Olmstead v. L.C. ex rel. Zimring,*[182] 527 U.S. 581, 597 (1999) ('Unjustified isolation . . . is properly regarded as discrimination based on disability.')"

"To establish a violation of the integration mandate, a plaintiff must prove that 'the State's treatment professionals have determined that community placement is appropriate, the transfer from institutional care to a less restrictive setting is not opposed by the affected individual, and the placement can be reasonably accommodated, taking into account the resources available to the State and the needs of others with mental disabilities.' *Olmstead, at 587.* Further, as a general matter, to recover damages on a claim brought under the ADA, a plaintiff must show that the violation claimed was either intentional or the product of deliberate indifference to the plaintiff's rights." [Caselaw cite omitted.]

"The district court held that damages are not available for violations of the integration mandate, but even assuming, arguendo, that a plaintiff may seek such damages, we agree with the district court's alternative holding that Frank's complaint nonetheless does not state a valid claim for relief because it fails to allege deliberate indifference."

"Although Frank asserts that Little Flower was an unnecessarily restrictive setting, she also affirmatively alleges that MF's father possessed custody of MF during all relevant periods and that he consented to Sachem's placement of MF in Little

---

[182] This is the same Zimring referenced in the 2016 *Cobb County* case and was a party in the landmark *Olmstead* SCOTUS case.

Flower.[183] Given that Frank does not dispute that MF's father, by virtue of the custody order, had authority to act on MF's behalf and that a claim under the integration mandate requires proof that the affected individual opposed placement in the restrictive setting, MF's father's consent precludes Frank from establishing that Sachem acted with deliberate indifference to MF's rights."

(Parent's attorney - William M. Brooks // School's attorney - David F. Kwee)

Outcome: School district prevailed.

RK v. Scott County Bd. of Ed.
6th Cir. 2016
Kentucky - 2/5/2016

In this 504 / ADA neighborhood school placement case, "R.K.'s parents believe that the Scott County school board discriminated against their diabetic son by moving him out of his neighborhood school to a different school that had a full-time nurse on staff. The district court granted summary judgment to the school board. We affirm."

"R.K. was diagnosed with Type-1 diabetes at the age of four."

"In March 2009, R.K.'s parents tried to enroll him in kindergarten for the coming school year at Eastern Elementary. . . After a series of meetings with R.K.'s parents, the school board concluded that R.K. should attend a school with a full-time nurse on staff. The school board . . . enrolled R.K. at Anne Mason."

"By second grade, R.K. was fully independent in using his insulin pump, so the school board enrolled him at Eastern as his parents requested. Two months into the school year, however, R.K.'s family moved to a different school zone."

"In the middle of the transfer dispute, R.K. (through his parents) sued . . . [claiming] that the school board violated the ADA, the Rehabilitation Act, the Fourteenth Amendment, and the Kentucky Civil Rights Act by sending him to Anne Mason. As remedies, [for KG and 1st grade] he sought injunctive relief and money damages. The district court granted summary judgment to the school board and the superintendent on all claims."

"The parties devote the bulk of their argument to whether R.K. has a substantive right to attend his neighborhood school. But the parties overlook another element of R.K.'s claims, which is whether he can obtain the remedies he seeks . . . money damages. . . under the ADA and the Rehabilitation Act. R.K. must show that the school board acted with 'deliberate indifference' towards his federally-protected rights."

"This is not a case where a school board ignored a student's request for help. Rather, the student's parents simply disagreed with the school as to whether a nurse was necessary to provide it. Thus, as a matter of law, R.K. is not entitled to damages on his federal claims."

Outcome: School district prevailed.

Oliver v. Hofmeister
OK State Supreme Court, 2016
Oklahoma - 2/16/2016

[**Wrightslaw note** - This is not a U.S. Court of Appeals case. We included it because the issue has been litigated in other states and is capable of repeat litigation elsewhere. It has a subtle implications regarding separation of church and state values and dollars funding religious schools such as in the 2nd Circuit NY *Montesa* case.[184]]

"Oklahoma taxpayers [Oliver and others] filed a declaratory judgment action [against Hofmeister, OK Supt. Instruction] seeking . . . to enjoin the payment of tuition to private sectarian schools alleging the 'Lindsey Nicole Henry Scholarships for Students with Disabilities Act' violates several articles of the Oklahoma Constitution."

"Although the Act is religion neutral, Taxpayers urge there is constitutional significance because there are more students attending sectarian private schools than non-sectarian. We disagree."

In Oklahoma, the Department funds the scholarship by direct payment to the parent who pays the private school.

---

[183] Contra, see the Ninth Circuit's *AG v. Paradise Valley* where, despite parent's consent to other placement under IDEA, such reliance of parent's consent was a violation of Section 504.

[184] *Montesa v. Schwartz + East Ramapo* - religion and private schools was an issue, although the nature of the litigation was quite different.

"The Department has no influence on which private school the parent chooses . . . or whether the scholarship payment is made to a private sectarian or non-sectarian school."

"It is the parent who then directs payment . . . this independence of choice by the parent breaks the circuit between government and religion."

"[T]he State is not actively involved in the adoption of sectarian principles or directing monetary support to a sectarian institution through this scholarship. . . The scholarship funded through the Act has no bearing on state control of churches. We are convinced that the scholarships funded by the Act have no adverse impact on the ability of churches to act independently of state control and to operate separately from the state."

"We are guided by our long-standing jurisprudence that a legislative act is presumed to be constitutional and 'will be upheld unless it is clearly, palpably and plainly inconsistent with the Constitution.' We hold the Oklahoma 'Lindsey Nicole Henry Scholarships for Students with Disabilities Act', a school voucher program limited to provide educational choices for children with disabilities, does not violate Article II, Section 5 of the Oklahoma Constitution."

(Taxpayer/Oliver's attorney - Frederick J. Hegenbart // OK Supt. of Instruction's attorney - Patrick R. Wyrick)

Outcome: State Board of Education prevailed.

JV v. Albuquerque Pub. Sch.
813 F.3d 1289 (10th Cir. 2016)
New Mexico - 2/19/2016

The parents sued, alleging an ADA violation because their child, a seven-year-old second grader, was handcuffed[185] during a behavioral outburst. The case was dismissed by the District Court and Court of Appeals.

"During two hours on the morning of November 14, 2011, C.V. disrupted his class, ran away from APS staff, kicked an APS social worker, and kicked and shot rubber bands at APS School Security Officer Xiomara Sanchez. To protect C.V. and others, Officer Sanchez handcuffed him to a chair. Before doing so, Officer Sanchez had called C.V.'s mother, who granted permission to restrain him, and repeatedly warned C.V. to calm down. Officer Sanchez was unaware of C.V.'s disability."

"C.V.'s parents ("Appellants") sued under Title II of the Americans with Disabilities Act ("ADA"), claiming APS denied C.V. a protected benefit and discriminated against him. The district court granted summary judgment to APS. Exercising jurisdiction under 28 U.S.C. § 1291, we affirm."

"Officer Sanchez asked M.Q. for permission to restrain C.V. M.Q. responded, "Yes." M.Q. apparently did not understand that Officer Sanchez was seeking permission to handcuff C.V. Rather, she thought that a trained member of C.V.'s behavioral intervention team would hug or hold him to calm him down."

"We affirm summary judgment on both ADA claims because Appellants failed to show that APS or any of its staff took action against C.V. by reason of his disability. Appellants have not otherwise shown a triable issue as to whether APS denied C.V. access to education or that APS intentionally discriminated against C.V., implemented policies that imposed a disparate impact on disabled students, or failed to act on a request or obvious need for a reasonable accommodation."

"Our role is not to opine on whether it was wrong to handcuff C.V. First, Appellants failed to show that APS handcuffed C.V. because of his disability. Further, as to their denial of benefit claim, Appellants fail to show C.V. was denied access to education. As to their discrimination claim, Appellants failed to show APS intentionally discriminated against C.V., implemented policies that imposed a disparate impact on disabled students, or failed to respond to a request or obvious need for a reasonable accommodation."

(Parent's attorney - Joseph P. Kenney // School's attorney - Emil J. Kiehne)

Outcome: School district prevailed.

[185] Compare this case to another 2016 Tenth Circuit case where a thirteen-year-old student burped in his class. That child did not have an IEP or Section 504 Plan. His attorney unsuccessfully alleged violations of the U. S. Constitution. Newest Supreme Court Justice Gorsuch wrote a strong dissent on behalf of the youngster. See *AM v. Holmes*.

Anaheim Union High Sch. Dist. v. JE
9th Cir. 2016
California - 2/22/2016

The parent "appeals the district court's award of attorney fees and costs" which are to "be based on rates prevailing in the community in which the action or proceeding arose for the kind and quality of services furnished."

"J.E. first argues that the district court abused its discretion by reducing the hourly rate requested by his attorney . . ." The Ninth Circuit noted that "the district court adequately explained its conclusion that rates above $400 per hour were on the high end of fees charged in the relevant market, and therefore not 'prevailing' as required by IDEA."

"J.E. next argues that the district court abused its discretion by denying his request for paralegal fees. Generally, paralegal fees are recoverable by prevailing parties in an IDEA action, however, 'prevailing parents may not recover the costs of experts or consultants.' *Arlington Cent. Sch. Dist. Bd. of Educ. v. Murphy*, 548 U.S. 291, 300 (2006). J.E. requested $16,650 in paralegal fees for the work of Dr. Susan Burnett."

"The district court determined that Dr. Burnett had worked as an expert or consultant in the case, not as a paralegal. That conclusion is amply supported by the record. Dr. Burnett was introduced as an educational consultant at the due process hearing and was identified as an advocate . . . [and billed] for tasks that are not typical of paralegals, such as reviewing J.E.'s educational assessments and Individualized Education Program goals. [The] declaration in support of her fee request states that Dr. Burnett meets the definition of paralegal in the California Business and Professions Code, but provides no evidence to support that assertion. Accordingly, the district court did not abuse its discretion in rejecting the claim for paralegal fees."

Outcome: School district prevailed.

Tina M. v. St. Tammany Parish Sch. Bd.
816 F.3d 57 (5th Cir. 2016)
Louisiana - 2/23/2016

In this "stay-put" and attorneys fee case, the Plaintiffs "brought suit on behalf of their minor son seeking attorneys' fees . . . [and the] district court held that Plaintiffs were the prevailing party by virtue of having obtained a 'stay-put' order under the IDEA and awarded Plaintiffs attorneys' fees. Because we hold that obtaining a stay-put order under the IDEA is not sufficient to qualify a litigant as a 'prevailing party,' we reverse."

The school district "convened an Individualized Education Program meeting where it proposed changing S.M.'s educational plan. Under this new plan, S.M. would no longer attend classes at the school but would instead receive at-home tutoring. S.M.'s mother disagreed with this proposal and refused to consent to the change."

". . . Plaintiffs' attorney requested a due process hearing regarding Defendant's decision to change S.M.'s educational program. . . Plaintiffs filed a memorandum of law arguing that pursuant to the IDEA's stay-put provision, S. M. should be permitted to attend classes at the school pending resolution of the dispute."

"[T]he Administrative Law Judge ('ALJ') issued a ruling granting Plaintiffs' request for a stay-put order. . . [directing] that S.M. be permitted to continue with his in-class educational program until a decision on the merits of the dispute was rendered. As the ALJ explained, '[u]nder [the] IDEA, a stay-put order is not a final adjudication of the merits of the issue of retention but serves as injunctive relief during the pendency of the due process action to maintain the status quo.'"

"Following this order, the parties reached a settlement through mediation, and Plaintiffs moved to terminate the pending administrative hearing on the merits. Pursuant to Plaintiffs' request, the ALJ terminated the matter and never reached the merits of Plaintiffs' claims."

"After the case was settled by agreement and without litigation, the Plaintiffs filed suit in the Eastern District of Louisiana seeking attorneys' fees . . . The parties disagreed as to whether Plaintiffs were entitled to attorneys' fees and filed cross-motions for summary judgment on the issue of whether Plaintiffs were the prevailing party."

"[T]he district court held that Plaintiffs were the prevailing party . . . and entered judgment for Plaintiffs. Defendant appeals the district court's holding that Plaintiffs are the prevailing party."

The Court of Appeals explained that the parents "must have 'obtained a judgment on the merits, a consent decree, or some similar form of judicially sanctioned relief.' (citing *Buckhannon Bd. & Care Home, Inc. v. W. Va. Dep't of Health & Human Res.*, 532 U.S. 598, 603-04 (2001)). Because the stay-put order issued by the ALJ does not satisfy this test, Plaintiffs are not the prevailing party and are not entitled to attorneys' fees."

"Contrary to the district court's conclusion, the ALJ's stay-put order was not a ruling on the merits. The IDEA's stay-put provision . . . guarantees an injunction that prohibits a school board from removing the child from his or her current placement during the pendency of the proceedings."

"Thus, when presented with an application for section 1415(j) relief, a district court should simply determine the child's then-current educational placement and enter an order maintaining the child in that placement. Indeed, the ALJ's order here, which repeatedly noted that 'the question of stay-put is procedural and not a determination on the merits of the case,' clearly reflects that there is no merits component to this analysis."

"Our holding that Plaintiffs are not the prevailing party by virtue of having invoked the IDEA's stay-put provision is consistent with several other circuit courts that have addressed this issue."

Outcome: School district prevailed.

AG v. Paradise Valley Unif. Sch. Dist.
815 F.3d 1195 (9th Cir. 2016)
Arizona - 3/3/2016
A Case of the Year for 2016

The Ninth Circuit reversed the Arizona District Court ruling and, in doing so, provided a very comprehensive review of the interplay and requirements of IDEA v. 504 and ADA, the different definitions of FAPE, and the Section 504 regulations.[186] Attorneys should read the full decision several times and not rely on this abridged version.[187]

The state court complaint filed in 2010 [and located on Wrightslaw[188] with the other pleadings] alleged state law torts of assault and battery, false imprisonment, and violations of Section 504 and ADA. The school district removed the case to federal court, which dismissed. On appeal, the Ninth Circuit reversed in favor of parents.

As background, the parents settled their IDEA failure to provide FAPE claim, and went forward on their 504 / ADA claim and their state law tort claims. A major issue was the child's change of placement from the "Uniquely Gifted Program for students with high IQs and one or more learning or behavioral disabilities" at Vista Verde Middle School to "the Roadrunner School, a school primarily designed for children with emotional disturbances." The Ninth Circuit explained that FAPE as defined by IDEA is quite different from the 504 / ADA definition and, even if the IDEA FAPE was sufficient, the 504 / ADA FAPE was not.

The Court begins this Opinion with: "This appeal implicates overlapping federal statutes addressing discrimination on the basis of disability. Specifically, we address the requirement that all children with disabilities receive a free appropriate public education ('FAPE'), and the distinct but overlapping features of FAPE set forth under the different statutory schemes. The related statutory schemes at issue here are . . ." [Legal cites omitted.]

It was alleged that the school failed to provide "adequate accommodations, including a Functional Behavior Assessment (FBA), a Behavior Intervention Plan (BIP), a full-time aide," and should not have changed A.G.'s placement from Vista Verde to the Roadrunner School, even though the parent consented to the change. "Plaintiffs alleged that having further accommodations would have allowed A.G. to continue attending Vista Verde."

---

186 **Section 504 Regulations**: http://www.wrightslaw.com/law/504/sec504.regs.linked.pdf

187 This case is a **Case of the Year for 2016** and is **required reading** for all attorneys litigating special ed claims.

188 www.wrightslaw.com/law/caselaw/2016/paradisevalley/

"Because remand is necessary, we clarify the relevant standards for disability discrimination claims [pursuant to Section 504 and ADA] by disabled children based on access to educational services."

The Court's outline contained two primary headers. The first one is titled "Federal Legislation Addressing Special Education for Disabled Children" and explained that "There are three primary and overlapping pieces of federal legislation applicable to plaintiffs' discrimination claims:" [IDEA, Section 504 + ADA] [Legal cites omitted.]

The second header is titled "The district court improperly dismissed A.G.'s meaningful access and reasonable accommodation arguments." Judge LeMelle then defined "Meaningful Access," "Reasonable Accommodation," and "Deliberate Indifference."

The Court explained that "Section 504 of the Rehabilitation Act is broader than the IDEA; it is concerned with discrimination in the provision of state services to all individuals with disabilities."

The 504 regulations require public schools to provide FAPE which "is defined differently for purposes of section 504 than it is for the IDEA. Under those section 504 regulations, FAPE requires 'regular or special education and related aids and services that (i) are designed to meet individual educational needs of handicapped persons as adequately as the needs of non-handicapped persons are met...' In other words, FAPE in the 504 setting means that the child receives education and services "as adequately" as provided to non-special ed children.

"Section 504's regulations gauge the adequacy of services provided to disabled individuals by comparing them to the level of services provided to individuals who are not disabled."

"A plaintiff bringing suit under section 504 or Title II of the ADA must show: she was denied a reasonable accommodation that [she] needs to enjoy meaningful access to the benefits of public services . . ."

The plaintiff can also show a denial of meaningful access "to public education through another means, such as by violating a regulation that implements section 504's prohibitions." [Cites omitted.]

"Finally, to prevail on a claim for damages under section 504 and Title II, 'plaintiffs must prove a mens rea of intentional discrimination . . . [and] that standard may be met by showing 'deliberate indifference, . . . not only by showing 'discriminatory animus.'" [Caselaw cites omitted.]

"Under our case law, '[d]eliberate indifference requires both knowledge that a harm to a federally protected right is substantially likely, and a failure to act upon that . . . likelihood.' [Caselaw cites omitted.] The plaintiff establishes the requisite knowledge (or notice) on behalf of the defendant when she shows that she 'alerted the public entity to [her] need for accommodation (or where the need for accommodation is obvious, or required by statute or regulation).'"

"Thus, a public entity can be liable for damages under § 504 if it intentionally or with deliberate indifference fails to provide meaningful access or reasonable accommodation to disabled persons.'" [Caselaw cites omitted.]

The Court then explained that "The district court improperly dismissed A.G.'s meaningful access and reasonable accommodation arguments."

"A. Meaningful Access" - "Plaintiffs claim that A.G.'s placement at Roadrunner denied her meaningful access because certain educational opportunities such as art, music, and gifted classes were not available at Roadrunner, and . . . because they failed to provide her appropriate behavioral supports and services at the two schools, as reflected in her allegedly deficient IEPs. Therefore, plaintiffs argue, A.G.'s educational opportunities at Vista Verde and Roadrunner were not 'as adequate as' those provided to her peers at Vista Verde." [Legal cite omitted.]

"Section 104.34 mandates that a disabled student be placed in the least restrictive 'regular educational environment' [LRE] and requires that school districts comply with various evaluative procedures and justify any changes in placement. [Legal cite omitted.] Plaintiffs argue that the school district transferred her to Roadrunner school without complying with § 104.34's procedural requirements, and that this transfer prevented her from accessing certain educational opportunities."

"The district court dismissed plaintiffs' meaningful access argument. In doing so, it appeared to reason that A.G.'s parents' consent to placement at Roadrunner waived the claim. The district court also ruled that A.G. was not 'qualified' to participate in the art, music, and gifted education classes of which she claimed to be deprived, because 'she had repeatedly refused to do so at Vista Verde.' Finally, the court noted that A.G.'s parents participated in the IEP team meetings where they had an opportunity to raise concerns that Roadrunner's behavioral policies were inappropriate for students diagnosed with autism."

"The district court's reliance on A.G.'s parents' consent was misplaced. We have previously held that claims challenging the placement of a disabled child are not barred simply because the parents of the child consent, or fail to object, to such placement. [Caselaw cites omitted.] The conclusion in *J.W.* arose from an IDEA claim rather than claims under section 504 or Title II, but we are persuaded that a claim that meaningful access has been improperly denied within the meaning of these latter statutes is not 'precluded or waived based on a parent's consent to an IEP,' at least where the issue is one that requires specialized expertise a parent cannot be expected to have."

"Because the district court relied on A.G.'s parents' consent[189] to placement at Roadrunner in dismissing plaintiffs' meaningful access claim without evaluating whether A.G.'s educational needs were met as adequately as those of her non-disabled peers, its decision must be reversed and remanded."

"B. Reasonable Accommodation" - "A plaintiff may establish prohibited discrimination . . . by showing that a public entity denied her a 'reasonable accommodation' necessary to achieve meaningful access to her education. . . [A] plaintiff must show that the 'defendant failed to make reasonable modifications that would accommodate the plaintiff's disability without fundamentally altering the nature of the program or activity,' and that the accommodation would have enabled her to meet the 'program's essential eligibility requirements.'" [Caselaw cites omitted.]

Parents argued that a "reasonable accommodation" would have included assigning her "a full time behavioral aide, to meaningfully access her education . . .[and] would have allowed A.G. to continue her education at Vista Verde rather than be transferred to Roadrunner. . . Defendants did not dispute in the district court or on appeal that a full-time aide could have been available."

"As a consequence, we conclude that a triable factual dispute exists as to whether the services plaintiffs fault the school district for failing to provide were actually reasonable, necessary, and available accommodations for A.G. Thus, summary judgment on this issue was improper." [Legal cite omitted.]

"C. Deliberate Indifference" - "Where, as here, the plaintiff seeks damages under section 504 and the ADA, she must show the defendant had notice of her need for an accommodation and 'fail[ed] to act.' She can establish notice by showing that she 'alerted the public entity to [her] need for accommodation;' or that 'the need for accommodation [was] obvious, or required by statute or regulation.' When an entity is on notice of the need for accommodation, it 'is required to undertake a fact-specific investigation to determine what constitutes a reasonable accommodation.'" [Caselaw cites omitted.]

The Court, ruling in the parent's favor, remanded the case back to the District Court for resolution of the state law torts of assault and battery and false imprisonment and the Section 504 and Title II ADA claims.[190]

COPAA filed an Amicus brief with the Court in this case.

(Parent's attorney - Richard J. Murphy // School's attorney - Erin H. Walz)

Outcome: Parents prevailed.[191]

[189] Contra, see Second Circuit's 2/3/2016 *Frank v. Sachem* where reliance on parent's consent was appropriate.

[190] After reading this case, we suggest that you read ***Parent and Educator Resource Guide to Section 504***, an excellent December 2016 OCR publication.

[191] **Update** - After the U.S. District Court scheduled the case for a Jury Trial, the case settled in November 2016.

LK v. Sewanhaka Cent. High Sch. Dist.
2nd Cir. 2016
New York - 3/4/2016

This case is a *Fry* failure to exhaust administrative remedies case.

In its dismissal, the Second Circuit explained that: "Plaintiffs L.K. and her daughters, N.S. and S.S., appeal from the dismissal of their complaint, charging defendants with disability discrimination and retaliation in violation of the Americans with Disabilities Act and Section 504 of the Rehabilitation Act."

"Although plaintiffs do not plead an IDEA violation, it is well settled that plaintiffs must exhaust administrative remedies under the IDEA 'whenever they assert claims for relief available under the IDEA, regardless of the statutory basis of their complaint, and that the failure to do so deprives the court of subject-matter jurisdiction. [Caselaw cite omitted.] Thus, if the 'theory' behind a claim relates to the 'education of disabled children,' IDEA exhaustion is required unless plaintiffs demonstrate that their failure to exhaust should be excused." [Caselaw cite omitted.]

"Here, plaintiffs do not dispute that they did not exhaust administrative remedies. Rather, they contend that this failure does not bar their ADA, Section 504, and Equal Protection claims because (1) the theory of their grievance goes 'beyond a simple dispute over the appropriate elements of" an individualized education program ("IEP") and, therefore, IDEA exhaustion is not required, and (2) even if the IDEA's exhaustion requirement applies, their failure should be excused. We are not persuaded."

"The theory behind plaintiffs' grievance is that N.S.'s and S.S.'s 'medical diagnoses have been used as the excuse to deny them the opportunity to receive an appropriate education since 2009.' Specifically, plaintiffs allege that after both children were diagnosed with chronic fatigue syndrome in 2009, defendants improperly denied their request for within-home schooling. Plaintiffs further allege that, although defendants granted that request in 2011, defendants' delay in doing so had by then caused N.S. and S.S. to lose two years of schooling, and defendants have failed to provide a way for N.S. and S.S. to graduate from high school before they turn 21 years old, at which point the school district will no longer be required to provide instruction."

"Further, under the IDEA, '[p]arents are specifically entitled to request a due process hearing to present complaints as to any . . . placement of the child, or the provision of free appropriate public education.' [Caselaw cite omitted.] Indeed, here, '[t]he administrative process would have been particularly valuable' in resolving plaintiffs' complaint that even when they did receive IEPs for homebound instruction, the IEPs failed to provide guidance as to how the curriculum could be modified to allow N.S. and S.S. to graduate before age 21. [Caselaw cite omitted.] Accordingly, the district court did not err in concluding that plaintiffs' ADA, Section 504, and Equal Protection claims are subject to the IDEA's exhaustion requirement."

(Parent's attorney - Steven A. Morelli // School's attorney - Mark A. Radi)

Outcome: School district prevailed, case dismissed.

Cripps v. Hurst-Euless-Bedford Indep. Sch. Dist.
5th Cir. 2016
Texas - 3/9/2016

A twelve-year old ADHD boy took a photograph of another student while she was sitting on the toilet. The Manifestation Determination Review committee held this behavior was not a manifestation of his disability, so he was placed into an alternative educational placement for 60 days.

"The parents filed a retaliation claim with the Office of Civil Rights, which determined that the Defendants had a legitimate reason for acting against CC and, thus, the retaliation claim failed. The Plaintiffs then filed a petition for a due process hearing under the IDEA, and the hearing officer dismissed each of the Plaintiffs' claims that was not brought under the statute. Following the hearing, the hearing officer issued an order upholding the District's decision."

"The Plaintiffs filed a complaint in the Northern District of Texas appealing the result of the due process hearing and alleging substantive and procedural due process violations, a violation of the equal protection clause, and violations of section 504 of the Rehabilitation Act. The Defendants filed a motion to dismiss the complaint for failure to state a claim upon which relief may be granted." The District Court dismissed the case.

"During oral argument, counsel clarified that the Plaintiffs limited their challenge to the district court's dismissal of their claims brought under section 504 of the Rehabilitation Act. . . The Plaintiffs also did not plead facts sufficient to establish that these behavioral infractions were the result of CC's ADHD."

In upholding the dismissal, the Court noted "The Plaintiffs did not sufficiently plead that any of the Defendants' acts were based on CC's disability; therefore, the Plaintiffs did not sufficiently plead that the Defendants violated § 504 by discriminating against CC."

Outcome: School district prevailed

Rockwall Indep. Sch. Dist. v. MC
816 F.3d 329 (5th Cir. 2016)
Texas - 3/10/2016

In this tuition reimbursement case, the hearing officer ruled in the parent's favor and awarded reimbursement for a private placement. Rockwall appealed to the district court which reversed and ruled in favor of the school district because it found that the parents had no intention of continuing with the ARDC[192] unless RISD approved their proposal to allow M.C. to remain at the private placement for the spring 2012 semester.

"When RISD sought to reschedule the follow-up ARDC, M.C.'s parents responded 'we do not believe that an ARD is necessary at this time' and explicitly refused to attend any subsequent meetings - despite the fact that all parties understood that no IEP had been finalized at the end of the December 2011 meeting and further discussions were necessary."

The school district argued that "the record here supports a finding that the parents acted 'unreasonably' during the IEP-development process, thus barring them from recovering tuition expenses under the IDEA regardless of whether RISD offered M.C. a FAPE." [Caselaw cite omitted.]

The Court of Appeals agreed, adding: "Indeed, as other Circuits have explained, '[t]he IDEA was not intended to fund private school tuition for the children of parents who have not first given the public school a good faith opportunity to meet its obligations.' [Caselaw cite omitted.] Commensurate with these principles, the IDEA and its implementing regulations specifically provide that an award of private school tuition 'may be reduced or denied . . . upon a judicial finding of unreasonableness with respect to actions taken by the parents.'"

"Although '[t]he development of an IEP is meant to be a collaborative project,' [Caselaw cite omitted.] the district court found that M.C.'s parents 'limited their own participation [in the IEP-development process] by adopting an all-or-nothing position,' viz., that M.C. should be re-enrolled in the DLC or else. As explained below, the record amply supports this finding."

The Court of Appeals upheld the District Court's reversal of the tuition reimbursement award because of the "unreasonable" all or nothing, position of the parents.

Outcome: School district prevailed.

JC v. NYC DOE
2nd Cir. 2016
New York - 3/16/2016

In this NYC tuition reimbursement case, parents prevailed at due process, the review officer reversed, on appeal the District Court affirmed the dismissal by the review officer, and the parents appealed to the Second Circuit. The Second Circuit applied the "*Burlington-Carter*" test.[193]

---

[192] Admission, Review, Discharge Committee, i.e., an IEP meeting.

[193] In 1993, author Pete Wright represented Shannon Carter before the U. S. Supreme Court, referenced above,

The Second Circuit outlined the process used in weighing a decision by a hearing officer vis a vis a review officer. "But where, as here, the IHO and SRO disagree, we defer to the reasoned conclusions of the SRO as the final state administrative determination.'"

"When parents unilaterally enroll their child in a private school, we apply the three-part *Burlington-Carter* test to determine whether they should be reimbursed. Under the test, we look at (1) whether the school district's proposed plan will provide the child with a free appropriate public education [FAPE]; (2) whether the parents' private placement is appropriate to the child's needs; and (3) a consideration of the equities."

"We conduct a two-part inquiry under the first prong of the *Burlington-Carter* test. 'At the first step, courts examine whether there were procedural violations of the IDEA, namely, whether the state has complied with the procedures set forth in the IDEA. [Caselaw cites omitted.] Courts then examine whether the IEP was substantively adequate, namely, whether it was reasonably calculated to enable the child to receive educational benefits.'"

"If an IEP is substantively inadequate, parents are 'automatically entitle[d] . . . to reimbursement. procedural violations, however, only [entitle a parent to reimbursement] if they 'impeded the child's right to a [FAPE], significantly impeded the parents' opportunity to participate in the decision-making process, or caused a deprivation of educational benefits." [Legal cite omitted.] 'Multiple procedural violations may cumulatively result in the denial of a FAPE even if the violations considered individually do not.'"

"'The failure to conduct an adequate FBA is a serious procedural violation because it may prevent the CSE[194] from obtaining necessary information about the student's behaviors, leading to their being addressed in the IEP inadequately or not at all.' Such a failure also 'seriously impairs substantive review of the IEP because courts cannot determine exactly what information an FBA would have yielded and whether that information would be consistent with the student's IEP.'"

"Failure to conduct an FBA . . . does not render an IEP legally inadequate under the IDEA so long as the IEP adequately identifies a student's behavioral impediments and implements strategies to address that behavior. [W]e find no error in the SRO's conclusion that the failure to conduct an FBA or develop a BIP did not deny C.C. a FAPE. Finally, we affirm the SRO's conclusion that these procedural violations did not cumulatively deny C.C. a FAPE."

(Parent's attorney - Tracey Spencer Walsh //School's attorney - Jonathon A. Popolow)

Outcome: School district prevailed.

EC v. Philadelphia Sch. Dist.

3rd Cir. 2016

Pennsylvania - 3/21/2016

Parents prevailed at the due process hearing and sought attorneys' fees. The school district appealed "the attorneys' fee award, arguing that the appellees' charged hours were excessive, the fee lodestar should be reduced to account for the appellees' degree of success, and the award should have taken into consideration the financial condition of the school district. We find these arguments unpersuasive and affirm the district court's ruling in whole."

"The school district next argues that we should reduce the fee lodestar because the parents were not successful on all of their claims . . . But as the Supreme Court has explained, a failure to succeed on every claim does not preclude a plaintiff from recovering full compensation."

"Finally, the Philadelphia School District argues that the district court should have reduced the fee award by fifteen percent to account for the 'distressed' financial condition of the school district - a 'special circumstance,' according to the school district . . . However, that concern can neither be visited upon the shoulders of these plaintiffs nor excuse the school district from its statutory obligation of paying the reasonable fees here."

(Parent's attorney - David Berney)

Outcome: Parents prevailed.

---

and, secured a unanimous decision in *Florence County Sch. Dist. IV v. Carter* (510 US 7).

[194] Committee on Special Education

BD v. DCPS
817 F. 3d 792 (DC Cir. 2016)
DC - 3/22/2016

In this compensatory education and enforcement case, the District of Columbia Court of Appeals explains that: "This case concerns a family's efforts to enforce a child's right under the Individuals with Disabilities Education Act to a 'free appropriate public education,' or FAPE. In administrative proceedings, a hearing officer determined that the District of Columbia Public Schools (DCPS) had denied the child a FAPE and ordered limited compensatory education. The parents sued, challenging the adequacy of the compensatory education award. They also sought to enforce other portions of the Hearing Officer's Decision that were favorable to them, as well as to require the District to secure a therapeutic residential placement. The district court granted summary judgment for the District. For the reasons set forth below, we affirm in part, reverse in part, and remand for further proceedings consistent with this opinion."

Compensatory Education - "When a hearing officer or district court concludes that a school district has failed to provide a student with a FAPE, it has broad discretion to fashion an appropriate remedy, which can go beyond prospectively providing a FAPE, and can include compensatory education. [Caselaw cites omitted.] [A]n award of compensatory education 'must be reasonably calculated to provide the educational benefits that likely would have accrued from special education services the school district should have supplied in the first place.' In other words, compensatory education aims to put a student like B.D. in the position he would be in absent the FAPE denial."

"An appropriate compensatory education award must 'rely on individualized assessments,' and . . . the remedy 'will produce different results in different cases depending on the child's needs.' In some cases, the award may consist of 'only short, intensive compensatory programs targeted at specific problems or deficiencies,' while in others the student may require 'extended programs, perhaps even exceeding hour-for-hour replacement of time spent without FAPE.' To fully compensate a student, the award must seek not only to undo the FAPE denial's affirmative harm, but also to compensate for lost progress that the student would have made."

This requires "a 'flexible approach' . . . and, a mechanical award of services identical to those wrongly denied is inappropriate. [In] this case . . . the Hearing Officer had an obligation either to fashion a compensatory education program to redress that harm or to provide an adequate explanation for his decision not to do so."

"[T]he Hearing Officer failed to address the broader question of how to put B.D. in the educational position he would be in but for the FAPE denial. The Decision's lack of reasoned explanation for its implicit conclusion that B.D. was only minimally harmed by the FAPE denial means that we owe it 'little deference.' . . . We shall thus reverse the district court's grant of summary judgment to the District on this count."

Enforcement and Remedy - "The Davises complain that the District failed, contrary to the Hearing Officer's order, to reimburse them for all of the tutoring and occupational therapy they provided for B.D. prior to the decision. The District contends that the Davises have failed to point to any statutory basis for an enforcement cause of action."

The Circuit Court explained "that neither section 1415(i)(2)(A) nor section 1331 provides a cause of action for parents seeking to enforce a favorable hearing officer decision. We leave for another day the viability of the alternative bases for such a cause of action."[195]

In this *BD v. DCPS* case, Judge Millett wrote a concurring opinion and explained that "Under the IDEA, any 'matter relating to the identification, evaluation, or educational placement of the child, or the provision of a free appropriate public education

[195] In 1999, this author, Pete Wright had a case where the school district refused to implement a due process decision and pay tuition reimbursement and prospective tuition. The parents filed an administrative complaint with the State Department of Education. The State refused to force the district to comply. A special education due process hearing was filed against the State seeking an Order requiring the State to pay the tuition since, by statute, the State is ultimately responsible under IDEA. The Order was granted, the parents prevailed, the ruling was upheld by the U.S. District Court, and attorneys' fees awarded. wrightslaw.com/law/caselaw/VASEA_white.pdf

to such child' can be the basis of a due process complaint and hearing. See 20 U.S.C. § 1415(b)(6) & (f)(1). In the federal government's view, a school district's failure to comply with a hearing officer's decision is such a matter. Thus, according to the Department of Education, parents who face a lack of compliance may be able to bring another due process complaint to enforce the prior decision and, if necessary, seek judicial review of any denial of needed relief in that proceeding."

COPAA filed an Amicus brief with the Court in this case.

(Parent's attorney - Diana M. Savit // School's attorney - Richard S. Love)

Outcome: Parents prevailed

SM v. Gwinnett County Sch. Dist.

11th Cir. 2016

Georgia - 3/24/2016

In this mainstreaming / least restrictive environment (LRE) case from Georgia, the Eleventh Circuit explained that "Plaintiffs' primary argument on appeal is that the district court and the ALJ erred in concluding that the School District had complied with the 'mainstreaming' or 'least restrictive environment' provision of the Individuals with Disabilities Education Act, 20 U.S.C. § 1412(a)(5)(A) . . . We conclude that the judgment of the district court should be affirmed for the reasons set out in the comprehensive order of the district court dated May 29, 2015."

"Our decision in *Greer v. Rome City Sch. Dist.*, 950 F.2d 688 (11th Cir. 1991) adopted a two-part test for determining compliance with the mainstreaming requirement of the Act: First, we ask whether education in the regular classroom, with the use of supplemental aids and services, can be achieved satisfactorily. . . If it cannot and the school intends to provide special education or to remove the child from regular education, we ask, second, whether the school has mainstreamed the child to the maximum extent appropriate." (quoting *Daniel R.R. v. State Bd. of Educ.*, 874 F.2d 1036, 1048 (5th Cir. 1989)."

"Plaintiffs argue that the district court erred in concluding that the School District satisfied the first prong of the *Greer* test. Plaintiffs' primary argument is that the School District erroneously concluded that S.M. could not be educated satisfactorily in the regular classroom because it failed to consider the full range of supplemental aids and services that would have enabled S.M. to be educated satisfactorily in the regular classroom. We agree with the district court (and the ALJ) that the School District and the IEP Team, with full participation of S.M.'s parents, did consider a full range of such options."

"We note that the IEP did provide for S.M. to be educated in the regular classroom for all of the school day except for classes involving the foundational skills of reading, writing and math. We note that supplementary aids and services were provided to enable this education in the regular classroom. For example, co-teaching was provided in the regular classroom setting for the subjects of science and social studies. The district court order lists a wide range of supplemental aids that were considered for feasibility, some of which were ultimately offered."

"We cannot disagree with the findings of the district court (and the ALJ) that the nature of S.M.'s special educational needs with respect to learning in reading, writing and math are such that she requires direct, explicit, small group instruction with drill and repetition, which instruction is significantly different from that of a general second grade classroom, such that S.M.'s education in these subjects could not be satisfactorily achieved in the regular classroom even with supplemental aids and services. We agree with the district court (and the ALJ) that the IEP places S.M. in the regular classrooms 'to the maximum extent appropriate' as required by the Act."

COPAA filed an Amicus brief with the Court in this case.

(Parent's attorney - Torin Togut)

Outcome: School district prevailed.

Rideau v. Keller Indep. Sch. Dist.

819 F. 3d 155 (5th Cir. 2016)

Texas - 4/5/2016

This case involved child abuse by the child's special education teacher. A jury awarded a one-million-dollar verdict against the school district. After the verdict, the district discovered that the incompetent adult child had a trust maintained by a bank. The district asserted that the parents did not have standing to sue. Only the bank trustee had standing.

"The district court held that the bank was the proper party and dismissed the claims rather than allow the bank to ratify the parents' actions pursuant to Federal Rule of Civil Procedure 17(a)(3). We are called upon to decide whether the parents were proper plaintiffs, and if not, whether the district court should have allowed ratification to correct the error."

As background, the Fifth Circuit explained that "In his early teen years, T.R. was a special education student at Keller Independent School District, during which time he was repeatedly mistreated by his special education teacher. The teacher's conduct ranged from petty slights (eating T.R.'s lunch) to dereliction of duties (not following key aspects of T.R.'s Individual Education Plan) to physical abuse (T.R. suffered a broken thumb, a dislocated knee, and skull contusions in the teacher's care)."

"Due to his disability, T.R. could not tell his parents what was happening, although his physical injuries and regression in life skills signaled that something was terribly wrong. The Rideaus lodged concerns with the school district. To their shock, they learned that a classroom aide had reported misconduct by the special education teacher years before, but that nothing had been done to remove, discipline, or fire the teacher in question."

The parents sued and a "jury awarded a substantial verdict. After trial, the school district challenged the verdict [arguing] that the parents were never the proper parties to bring these claims in the first place." The District Court agreed, struck the verdict. The parents and the bank trustee appealed to the Fifth Circuit.

"In a private dispute such as this one, the question of who should sue typically has an obvious answer. But the answer was complicated here by a number of factors: the victim was a minor when the challenged conduct occurred but turned 18 by the time of trial; his disability rendered him incompetent even after he reached majority; a bank had been appointed to serve as his guardian; and that same bank oversaw a trust that paid for the minor's medical bills. The school district's argument that the bank should have brought the suit was not raised until after trial because evidence relating to the bank's role was not disclosed pretrial."

The Court of Appeals noted that, as "a general rule, when a person has been declared to be incapacitated and a guardian has been appointed, only the guardian of the ward's estate may bring a lawsuit on behalf of the ward. . ."

"[T]he district court appeared to accept that a mistake was made but did not accept that it was understandable. The court's finding of no understandable mistake cannot withstand even deferential scrutiny. The Rideaus did provide an explanation for PlainsCapital's omission: they believed that they too could bring their son's claims."

"On another note, shifting from the standing issue and who must file suit, the Court also addressed whether the Rideaus can recover mental anguish damages based on the mistreatment of their disabled son, we find that neither the ADA nor the Rehabilitation Act authorizes such claims."

The Fifth Circuit affirmed "the dismissal of the Rideaus' individual mental anguish claims [but vacated the rest of] "the judgment entered by the district court in favor of Keller ISD. We reverse the denial of PlainsCapital's motion to ratify the actions of the Rideaus and to be bound by the judgment and remand for further proceedings consistent with this opinion."

The jury verdict form noted that $150,000 was for the mental anguish suffered by the parents. Thus, the award was reduced by that amount from $1,000,000 to $850,000.

(Parent's attorney - John Franklin Guild // School's attorney - Thomas Phillip Brandt)

Outcome: Parents prevailed.

SB v. Harford County Bd. of Ed.
819 F. 3d 69 (4th Cir. 2016)
Maryland - 4/8/2016

Parents argued that their child, S.B., was bullied because of his disability. The stepfather, T.L., who worked in the same school, also asserted that, in violation of Section 504, the school district retaliated against him because of his advocacy on behalf of S.B.

"After extensive discovery, the district court granted summary judgment to the Board, holding that there was no record evidence to support either S.B.'s or T.L.'s claims. And while we sympathize with students and parents who face school bullying issues, we agree. S.B. has provided no evidence that the Board acted with the deliberate indifference necessary to hold it liable for student-on-student harassment. Nor does the record substantiate T.L.'s allegation of a causal connection between his advocacy for S.B. and any adverse action taken by the Board. Accordingly, we affirm the judgment of the district court."

"Specifically, regarding S.B.'s claim of disability-based discrimination, the district court first found that 'it is not at all clear that any harassment directed toward [S.B.] was on account of his disability.' But the district court rested its decision on a different ground: that there was 'absolutely no evidence' in the record that the Board had discriminated against S.B. by acting with 'bad faith, gross misjudgment or deliberate indifference in responding to' student-on-student harassment. Instead, the record showed that the 'Board investigated every harassment claim against S.B. brought to its attention and assigned a person to be with S.B. throughout the school.' As to T.L.'s retaliation claim, the district court concluded that there was 'no evidence whatsoever' of a causal link between T.L.'s advocacy of S.B.'s rights and any action taken by the Board."

"[The] deliberate indifference standard requires a plaintiff like S.B. to show that he was an individual with a disability, harassed by fellow students based on his disability; that the disability-based harassment was sufficiently 'severe, pervasive, and objectively offensive' that it effectively deprived him of 'access to educational benefits and opportunities' at school, *Davis*, 526 U.S. at 650; and that the school knew about the disability-based student-on-student harassment and was deliberately indifferent to it. [Caselaw cite omitted.] Like the district court, we conclude that on the record evidence in this case, no reasonable jury could find that S.B. has made the necessary showing."

"Moreover, though there is no question but that the school was on notice that S.B. was being bullied, there is very much a question as to whether the school knew of any disability-based bullying, as would be required for S.B. to prevail under the *Davis* standard.[196] Even assuming that S.B. was on occasion harassed because of his disability, none of the email communications or harassment reports filed by S.B. or his parents and included in the record informed the school of that fact. S.B. argues that the school should have known, by way of investigation, that the harassment of which he complained was based on his disability..."

"Thus, it is not enough that a school has failed to eliminate student-on-student harassment, or to impose the disciplinary sanctions sought by a victim. [Caselaw cite omitted.] Instead, a school will be liable for student-on-student harassment only where its 'response . . . or lack thereof is clearly unreasonable in light of the known circumstances.' [Caselaw cite omitted.]

The Fourth Circuit upheld the District Court finding of an insufficient Section 504 legal basis regarding both the bullying of the child and retaliation claim by the stepfather.

COPAA filed an Amicus brief with the Court in this case.

(Parent's attorney - Martin Jay Cirkiel // School's attorney - Andrew G. Scott)

Outcome: School prevailed.

R. M-G v. Bd. of Ed. Las Vegas NM City Sch
10th Cir. 2016
New Mexico - 4/13/2016

In this ESY, O&M, comp ed and attorney fee case, the parents prevailed in two separate actions. The school district appealed each to the District Court which combined the cases and awarded full fees and "fees on fees" to the parent's attorney. This award was upheld by the Tenth Circuit.

"A.R. is legally blind and suffers from a congenital bone disorder characterized by brittle bones. He is a student in the Las Vegas City School

[196] *Davis v. Monroe County Bd. of Ed.*, 526 U.S. 629 (1999)

District and requires special educational instruction and services, including Braille instruction, orientation and mobility (O&M) services, and extended school-year (ESY) services."

"In November 2012, Parent requested a due-process hearing with the New Mexico Public Education Department. She complained (through counsel) that the District had 'not developed or implemented IEPs . . . that adequately addresse[d] [A.R.'s] needs for specialized instruction,' and had not provided O&M services."

"A hearing officer conducted a three-and-a-half day hearing, during which fifteen witnesses testified. After the hearing, the officer ruled that the District had failed to provide A.R. a free and appropriate education (FAPE) by not providing (1) ESY services in the summer following fourth grade; (2) ESY services in the summer following fifth grade; and (3) O&M services in the first semester of sixth grade. To remedy the deprivation of FAPE, the hearing officer ordered the District to 'provide [A.R.] with compensatory education in the form of comprehensive summer programming.' Specifically, the hearing officer 'awarded two summers (2013 and 2014) in. . . an overnight, support program for the blind and visually impaired,' with each program 'last[ing] a minimum of six weeks.' "

"As a result of the hearing officer's award, 'A.R. attended the Colorado Center for the Blind for two summers for 8 weeks each summer.' In addition to each program's $7,600 cost, the District paid A.R.'s transportation costs."

"[T]he hearing officer chastised the District for its 'cavalier attitude toward the services required to meet [A.R.'s] needs,' noting that '[e]ven though [A.R.] has progressed and improved his Braille fluency while in District's program, he is still two years below grade,' which 'is impacting his access to the academic curriculum.'"

The Tenth Circuit advised, "Where the parent 'has obtained excellent results, [the] attorney should recover a fully compensatory fee,' and there should be no reduction in the award 'simply because [the parent] failed to prevail on every contention.' [Caselaw cite omitted.] ([S]tating that 'when a plaintiff achieves the principal goal of her lawsuit, lack of success on some of her interrelated claims may not be used as a basis for reducing the plaintiff's fee award). [O]n the other hand, [if] [a parent] has achieved only partial or limited success, the product of hours reasonably expended on the litigation as a whole times a reasonable hourly rate may be an excessive amount.' *Hensley*, 461 U.S. at 436."

The Tenth Circuit upheld the District Court's award of fees on fees and closed with "Finally, because Parent may be entitled to recover attorney fees for prevailing on appeal, we remand for the district court to determine whether such fees are warranted, and if so, the amount of those fees."

Outcome: Parents prevailed.

Se.H v. Anne Arundel Bd. of Ed.
4th Cir. 2016
Maryland - 5/2/2016

"The ALJ for the Maryland Office of Administrative Hearings (OAH) found the following facts, which are undisputed on appeal. Se.H. has been diagnosed with several medical conditions, including cerebral palsy; severe food allergies to wheat/gluten, barley, peanuts, and buckwheat; allergies to dust, pollen, mold, and smoke; asthma, including Baker's Asthma (an allergic disease caused mainly by inhalation of flour); oral dysphasia (a swallowing disorder) and feeding difficulties; dysarthria (a weakening of speech-producing muscles); seizure disorder; postural kyphosis (an abnormal curve of the spine); and vision problems . . ."“Se.H.'s parents are dissatisfied with the IEP . . . because it does not require that an individual trained in Heimlich and CPR is by Se.H.'s side at all times throughout the day." They requested a special education due process hearing.

"Apart from attorney's fees and costs, Appellants seek only the following equitable relief: an order requiring the Aide to be trained in Heimlich and CPR, and a declaratory judgment stating that AACPS's Section 504 practices violate Section 504 as applied to Se.H."

The ALJ "ruled the Individuals with Disabilities Education Act does not entitle Se.H., who was a first grader during the 2013-14 school year, to an individual trained in Cardiopulmonary Resuscitation (CPR) and the Heimlich maneuver to accompany him throughout the school day."

The parents unsuccessfully appealed to the district court which noted that: "It is true that because of Se.H.'s physical condition, there is a greater risk he will need CPR or the administration of the Heimlich maneuver than other students. However, [AACPS] has in place reasonable procedures to assure that if Se.H. does need assistance, there are persons available who will be able to help him. One certainly is sympathetic to Se.H. and his parents. However, reasonableness is something less than perfection, and, as found by the [ALJ], the measures that defendant has put in place provide adequate protection of Se.H."

"The district court upheld this decision. Appellants contend the district court erroneously deferred to the ALJ's IDEA decision, and also failed to address their claims under Section 504 . . . and Title II of the [ADA]."

"We hold that the district court properly granted summary judgment in favor of Appellees on Appellants' IDEA claims. However, the district court's reasons for disposing of the Section 504 and ADA claims are unclear. Therefore, we remand to allow the district court to clarify the reasoning underlying its disposition of these claims."

In a footnote, the Fourth Circuit noted: "Se.H. attended kindergarten at Rippling Woods during the 2012-13 school year, and during that year, as well as 2013-14, he had no episodes of choking or anaphylaxis, did not require administration of the Heimlich maneuver or CPR, and had no episodes requiring a 911 call. Se.H. had not attended any field trips at the time of the ALJ's hearing."

COPAA filed an Amicus brief with the Court in this case.

(Parent's attorney - Selene Almazan-Altobelli // School's attorney - Manisha Sharad Kavadi)

Outcome: School district prevailed on IDEA IEP issue, but case remanded regarding 504 / ADA issues.

JS v. NYC DOE
2nd Cir. 2016
New York - 5/4/2016

In this tuition reimbursement case, the parents lost at Due Process, lost at Review, lost before the District Court, and appealed to the Second Circuit.

"The IHO, SRO, and district court all agreed that the IEP provided D.S. with a FAPE. Appellants disagree and argue that the Integrated Co-Teaching (ICT) placement in the IEP was not appropriate considering D.S.'s disabilities."

"The main issues in dispute at the independent hearing was whether D.S. had made enough progress to join an ICT classroom. This is exactly the type of educational policy question on which courts generally defer to hearing officers because it requires 'specialized knowledge and experience.' "

"We find, therefore, that the SRO's decision was 'reasoned and supported by the record,' and we defer to its findings that Appellee provided D.S. with a FAPE." [Caselaw cite omitted.]

"Because we find that D.S.'s IEP was appropriate, we need not address whether Appellants' private placement was appropriate or whether the equitable factors favor reimbursement. [Caselaw cite omitted.] We have considered all of Appellants' remaining arguments and find them to be without merit. The decision of the district court is AFFIRMED."

(Parent's attorney - Beth E. Goldman // School's attorney - Kathy Chang Park)

Outcome: School district prevailed.

HB v. Byram Hills Cent. Sch. Dist.
2nd Cir. 2016
New York - 5/6/2016

This is another *Fry* "Failure to Exhaust Administrative Remedies" case.

The Second Circuit noted that the "Appellants contend that exhaustion was futile because of the significant delays they experienced awaiting decision from an impartial hearing officer (IHO). While we acknowledge the lengthy delay, the fact remains that on August 20, 2014, Appellants and the Byram Hills School District (the District) both agreed to extend the deadline for a decision by the IHO until October 6, 2014, so that the newly-appointed IHO would have time to review the record."

"[T]he delay here is unlikely to recur because it was caused by a unique set of circumstances: an IHO's medical condition and the recusal of subsequent IHOs. It also bears noting that the IHO who caused the initial delay is no longer certified to be an IHO."

"Only two days after agreeing to this deadline, however, Appellants filed this lawsuit. While we have acknowledged that exhaustion may be futile if 'administrative bodies persistently fail to render expeditious decisions as to a child's education placement,' [Caselaw cite omitted.] as of the date this suit was filed, the wheels had been set in motion to resolve the delay that had occurred and to render a decision in the coming weeks. Moreover, the mutually agreed upon October deadline strongly suggested that a decision was imminent and that exhaustion, at least at that stage of proceedings, was not futile. Indeed, the IHO rendered a decision on October 15, 2014, less than two weeks after the agreed deadline. Under these circumstances, we agree with the district court that Appellants did not meet their burden to show that exhaustion would have been futile." [Caselaw cite omitted.]

The parents failed to exhaust their administrative remedies prior to filing suit in federal court so their case was dismissed.

(Parent's attorney - Peter D. Hoffman // School's attorney - Andrea Green)

Outcome: School district prevailed.

MS v. Utah Sch. for Deaf and Blind
822 F. 3d 1128 (10th Cir. 2016)
Utah - 5/10/2016

This is a compensatory education, placement and improper delegation of judicial authority case. M.S. is a residential student at the Utah Schools for the Deaf and Blind (USDB), is blind, hearing impaired and has been diagnosed with autism and a cognitive impairment.

"Believing USDB . . . was not providing M.S. with a FAPE, [his mother], J.S. sought a due process hearing. Unsatisfied with the limited relief she obtained in that hearing, J.S. filed a civil action in federal court. J.S. now appeals from the district court decision granting her additional limited relief. She asserts the district court erred when it (1) delegated its authority to resolve the propriety of M.S.'s residential placement to members of the team tasked with developing M.S.'s individualized education program (IEP) . . ."

"On January 8, 2013, J.S. filed for a due process hearing, alleging USDB had committed procedural and substantive violations of IDEA. Another IEP meeting was scheduled for February 4, 2013; the December 17, 2012, IEP was finalized at that meeting. The 2012-13 IEP rejected J.S.'s request that M.S. be placed at Perkins and, instead, changed M.S.'s placement to the Provo School District."

"The hearing officer found that USDB predetermined extended-school-year services for M.S. outside of the context of an IEP meeting during 2011 and 2012 (i.e., denied summer language services without parental input or a decision from M.S.'s IEP team). To remedy this violation, the hearing officer ordered compensatory education in the form of direct speech-language-pathology services. The hearing officer also determined the Provo School District was not an appropriate placement for M.S. The hearing officer ruled in USDB's favor on all other claims raised by J.S."

On appeal by the mother, the "district court concluded that multiple failures on the part of USDB to properly implement the 2011-12 IEP denied M.S. a FAPE. . . concluded J.S. had carried her burden of demonstrating the Provo School District was not an appropriate placement for M.S . . . [and] concluded USDB committed a substantive violation of IDEA when it refused to reimburse J.S. for the travel costs associated with the Perkins IEE."

"Rather than order a specific placement, the [District] Court will require particular educational compensatory services to be offered to M.S. M.S.'s IEP team can then determine placement at an appropriate residential school that will provide her with the services ordered. This way, M.S.'s IEP team, the people most familiar with M.S. and with USDB's services, can determine if USDB or Perkins is an appropriate placement for M.S."

"J.S. asserts the district court erred in delegating to M.S.'s IEP team the decision whether to place M.S. at Perkins . . ."

This was the issue of the case, the entity that dropped the ball was told to pick it up and handle it appropriately, leaving the parent mistrustful and dissatisfied. The Court of Appeals sided with the parent.

"The record leaves no doubt that the district court delegated the question of whether M.S. should be placed at Perkins to M.S.'s IEP team."

"Here, the district court refused outright to resolve the placement issue, leaving the matter entirely to the discretion of the IEP team on remand. USDB has not cited, and this court has not found, a single case approving the wholesale remand by a district court to an IEP team of a properly exhausted request for compensatory services following a determination that a covered student had been denied a FAPE."

"In analogous circumstances, however, two circuits have held that IDEA does not allow the kind of delegation at issue in this case. Both the Sixth and D.C. Circuits have held that IDEA does not allow an IEP team to assume the authority given a hearing officer."

"Allowing the educational agency that failed or refused to provide the covered student with a FAPE to determine the remedy for that violation is simply at odds with the review scheme set out at § 1415(i)(2)(C)."

"This court thus concludes that the district court did, indeed, delegate the issue of M.S.'s placement to M.S.'s IEP team. We further conclude that such delegation is at odds with the review scheme set out in 20 U.S.C. § 1415. [Caselaw cite omitted.] Thus, we must remand this case to the district court to vacate its order and to resolve in the first instance whether M.S. should be placed at Perkins to compensate for USDB's failure to provide her with a FAPE."

(Parent's attorney - Chantel L. Alberhasky // School's attorney - Bridget K. Romano)

Outcome: Parents prevailed.

Douglas v. CA OAH v. JC + Cupertino Sch. Dist.9th Cir. 2016
California - 5/13/2016

The Ninth Circuit reversed the District Court, noting "this case presents a complex, challenging issue of first impression under California law."

In California, occupational services (OT), if medically necessary, may be provided to children with chronic needs by California Children's Services (CCS), part of the California Department of Health Care Services [HCS]. That Department, through its Director (Douglas) sued the California Office of Administrative Hearings, [OAH] the parents of a child with special needs, and the Cupertino Union School District and the Santa Clara County Office of Education.

HCS "shall determine whether a [CCS] eligible pupil, or a pupil with a private medical referral, needs medically necessary occupational therapy . . . [and CCS is] responsible for the provision of medically necessary occupational therapy . . . by reason of medical diagnosis and when contained in the child's individualized education program."

"By comparison, qualified personnel from local education agencies are to provide related services that are not deemed to be medically necessary by [HCS] but that the child's IEP team 'determines are necessary to assist a child to benefit from special education.' [HCS] 'shall determine whether a CCS eligible pupil, or a pupil with a private medical referral, needs medically necessary occupational therapy.'"

"[W]hat is less clear is whether parents who disagree with CCS's determination can seek review of that decision in a due process hearing under California's implementation of [IDEA], [HCS] argues that . . . review of that decision is the prerogative of CCS, and an Administrative Law Judge (ALJ) presiding over a due process hearing lacks jurisdiction to review the question. CCS has its own appeal procedure by which a parent can choose a doctor (among three selected by CCS) to review CCS's initial medical necessity determination."

"Several provisions of California law lead us to conclude that a parent may initiate a due process hearing to seek review of CCS's determination of medical necessity in a child's IEP . . . parents may request a due process hearing to review a department's failure to provide a related service required pursuant to § 7575 and specified in the child's IEP. CCS is not therefore beyond the jurisdiction of an ALJ."

"[O]ccupational therapy services in a child's IEP - whether medically or educationally necessary - are 'related services' over which an ALJ has jurisdiction in a due process hearing."

"[A]ll state departments are governed by the IDEA's procedural safeguards and disputes over 'related services' are to be resolved in due process hearings. A "related service" is defined to include occupational therapy . . . to assist an individual with exceptional needs to benefit from special education." [Legal cites omitted.]

"Occupational therapy services deemed to be medically necessary by CCS are necessary 'to assist an individual with exceptional needs to benefit from special education,' id., when they form part of the child's IEP. The purpose of an IEP is to set out measurable academic goals to meet the child's educational needs and for the child to make educational progress. [Legal cite omitted.] If medically necessary occupational therapy services were not also necessary for a child to benefit from special education, they would need not be included in the child's IEP . . ."

"Because the medically necessary occupational therapy services in J.C.'s IEP were necessary for him to benefit from special education, the ALJ also had authority to order compensatory therapy. [Caselaw cite omitted.] For the same reason, the ALJ had authority to order reimbursement for the independent assessments obtained by J.C.'s parents" [Legal cite omitted.]

"Finally, we acknowledge that this case presents a complex, challenging issue of first impression under California law. A case presenting a similar issue is currently pending before the California Court of Appeal. [Caselaw cite omitted.] Ordinarily, we might consider deferring submission or certifying the question to the California Supreme Court. However, we decided the case in the interest of judicial expediency and J.C.'s need for resolution."

Outcome: Parents, school districts, and OAH prevailed against HCS and CCS.

LO v. NYC DOE
822 F. 3d 95 (2nd Cir. 2016)
New York - 5/20/2016

LO v. NYC DOE is a **2016 Case of the Year.**

This case involved three years of IEPs, BIPs / FBAs, procedural violations, and a host of other issues. The plaintiffs lost at due process, lost at review, lost in District Court, and won big before the Second Circuit with a comprehensive detailed opinion that, much like *AG v. Paradise Valley Unified School District* by the Ninth Circuit, should be required reading for all spec ed attorneys.

"Before the court is an action brought under the Individuals with Disabilities Education Act by Plaintiff-Appellant L.O., on behalf of herself and her son, K.T., now a twenty-year-old autistic child, against Defendant-Appellee the New York City Department of Education (DOE). This appeal concerns L.O.'s challenge to the adequacy of three individualized education programs (IEP), which were characterized by a pattern of procedural violations of the IDEA committed by the DOE, and whether these errors deprived K.T. of a free appropriate public education (FAPE) for a period of three consecutive years."

"In December 2009, the DOE convened a local Committee on Special Education (CSE) meeting to develop an IEP for K.T. for the 2010 academic year. K.T. enrolled in the IEP's prescribed placement and continued to attend as provided for by two subsequent IEPs in December 2010 and March 2011, until he began refusing to attend school in November 2011. Thereafter, L.O. filed a due process complaint against the DOE, claiming procedural and substantive violations of the IDEA, and that K.T. had been deprived of a FAPE for the 2009-2010, 2010-2011, and 2011-2012 school years. Specifically, L.O. sought, among other things, the completion of further evaluations, program modifications, compensatory services, and attorney's fees and costs."

"Following a five-day hearing, an impartial hearing officer (IHO) denied L.O. that relief. L.O. appealed to a state review officer (SRO) who affirmed that decision. Thereafter, L.O. brought suit in the United States District Court for the Southern District of New York (Gardephe, J.), which affirmed the order of the SRO. See *L.O. v. N.Y.C. Dep't of Educ.*, 94 F. Supp. 3d 530, 537 (S.D.N.Y. 2015). L.O. appealed, contending primarily that the three IEPs formulated for K.T. violated the IDEA and deprived him of a FAPE. For the reasons set forth below, we REVERSE."

As one of the issues regarding the child's December 2009 IEP, the Court explained that "K.T.'s behaviors seriously interfered with instruction, the IEP required the development of a behavioral intervention plan (BIP), which . . . did not, however, attempt to identify the root causes of K.T.'s problem behaviors. Nor did the CSE request or develop a functional behavior assessment (FBA)."

The following year, the December 2010 IEP services remained "unchanged from the prior year and . . . a BIP nearly identical to that developed for K.T. for the prior school year. K.T. continued to attend his public school placement under the new IEP at PS 811X."

The parent requested a reevaluation and the CSE reconvened to review the child's IEP and ". . . recommended that K.T.'s services remain unchanged from the December 2011 IEP and that he continue his placement in the alternative assessment program and receive the same speech, physical, and occupational therapy services."

"The March 2011 IEP provided no new annual goals or short-term objectives, included a transition plan identical to that contained in the December 2010 IEP, and, although the March 2011 IEP stated that a new BIP had been developed for K.T., none was incorporated in the IEP. Thereafter, K.T. continued to attend the 6:1:1 public school placement until November 18, 2011, when he began refusing to attend school."

"On December 9, 2011, L.O. filed a due process complaint, claiming that the DOE had failed to provide K.T. with a FAPE for the 2009-2010, 2010-2011, and 2011-2012 school years. L.O. alleged eighteen separate deficiencies in the IEPs developed for K.T., including that

(1) the IEPs failed to reflect reliance on any evaluations or assessments of K.T.,

(2) the CSE created BIPs without the benefit of FBAs resulting in his refusal to attend school,

(3) the DOE failed to provide adequate speech-language services,

(4) the CSE failed to develop annual goals that adequately addressed K.T.'s educational needs,

(5) the IEPs failed to provide parent counseling and training as a related service, and

(6) K.T.'s significant deterioration as a result of inappropriate programming led to the need for a residential private school placement."

"On January 10, 2012, a five-day impartial hearing commenced before an IHO, which heard testimony from nine witnesses. On April 18, 2012, the IHO rejected L.O.'s challenge to the appropriateness of K.T.'s December 2009, December 2010, and March 2011 IEPs, and denied L.O.'s claim for relief."

"L.O. appealed the IHO's decision to an SRO. On March 15, 2013, the SRO affirmed the IHO's decision and dismissed the appeal, concluding that all three IEPs were properly designed to address K.T.'s educational needs."

"Thereafter, L.O. brought this action in the District Court, claiming procedural and substantive violations under the IDEA resulting in the denial of a FAPE for K.T, and seeking a reversal of the SRO's decision . . . the District Court, relying heavily on the SRO's analysis, affirmed that decision."

"Here, L.O. alleges that the DOE committed multiple procedural errors in formulating each of K.T.'s IEPs, independently and cumulatively resulting in the denial of a FAPE for each school year."

The Court of Appeals explained that "L.O. contends that the DOE's development of BIPs without available FBAs amounts to a serious violation of the IDEA's procedures and resulted in a FAPE deprivation for K.T. Specifically, she maintains that the omission of FBAs prevented the DOE from identifying and thus eliminating the factors actually causing K.T.'s interfering behaviors. . . [T]he SRO's conclusion that the IEPs were adequate in this regard was error."

"Further, as prescribed by the regulations, determining the cause of a handicapped child's problem behaviors is a minimum requirement. ('Behavioral intervention plan means a plan that is based on the results of an FBA and, at a minimum, includes . . . global and specific hypotheses as to why the problem behavior occurs . . .') That is, although each IEP contained a BIP, neither attempted to identify the root causes of these behavioral deficiencies so that they could be properly addressed and treated . . . the December 2009 IEP notes that the CSE and K.T.'s service providers did not know why K.T. displayed these interfering behaviors. ('Often times, [K.T.'s] mood and personality change without the staff or teacher realizing the antecedent behavior or underlying cause. At times he appears happy, while during other times, he appears upset, anxious, irritated, and frustrated . . . He can be verbally and physically aggressive, many times for no apparent reason.') Had an FBA been conducted, the CSE might have been able to identify what caused K.T. to behave in certain ways, and provide effective treatment for these behaviors."

"Moreover, the March 2011 IEP's deficiencies are aggravated by the fact that, in addition to the absence of an FBA, no BIP was developed for K.T. Although the SRO observed that K.T.'s interfering behaviors remained unchanged from the previous IEP and that no BIP was developed, the SRO reached no conclusion regarding whether this omission constituted a procedural error, a deprivation of a FAPE, or any error at all."

"Indeed, the IEP itself indicates that the CSE believed that a BIP was warranted, yet the CSE failed to follow through with its own directive."

"Further, we have repeatedly stated that the 'failure to conduct an FBA is a particularly serious procedural violation for a student who has significant interfering behaviors.' See *R.E.*, 694 F.3d at 194. Because the CSE failed to address the root causes of K.T.'s behavioral deficiencies, we are unable to determine whether the IEPs adequately identified K.T.'s behavioral impediments and whether the strategies formulated to address those behaviors were appropriate. Accordingly, the omission of FBAs in each IEP and the absence of a BIP in the March 2011 IEP constituted serious procedural violations impairing our ability to review the adequacy of the IEP provisions."

"[A]lthough we have not previously considered whether failure to comply with the speech-language therapy provision for students with autism might rise to the level of a FAPE deprivation, we are of the view that such an inadequacy constitutes a serious violation of the procedures of the IDEA. This is because central to the provision of a student's special education is his or her communicative functioning, including speech and language instruction."

"Accordingly, the DOE's procedural error in this case was a serious one and, contrary to the findings of the District Court, was not rehabilitated in the IEP by other provisions made by the CSE. The procedural error thus deprived K.T. of important educational benefits to which he was entitled by law."

"We have previously held that '[m]ultiple procedural violations may cumulatively result in the denial of a FAPE even if the violations considered individually do not.' [Caselaw cite omitted.] The District Court concluded, despite finding multiple procedural violations, that these errors, together, did not deny K.T. a FAPE. We disagree and find that, at a minimum, the errors we have identified in each IEP cumulatively resulted in a denial of a FAPE for

K.T. for the 2009-2010, 2010-2011, and 2011-2012 school years."

"There were four procedural violations present in each of the three IEPs, three of which we identified as serious errors in formulating K.T.'s public school program."

"First, there was no record evidence that the CSE reviewed any evaluative materials in developing any of K.T.'s IEPs. This was a clear violation of the IDEA and its implementing regulations, and it raised serious questions about the CSE's review of K.T.'s needs and the adequacy of its determinations in reaching the terms of the IEPs."

"Second, the CSE failed to conduct an FBA for any of the IEPs, despite finding that K.T. possessed behaviors that interfered with learning, which this Court has previously found to constitute 'a serious procedural violation because it may prevent the CSE from obtaining necessary information about the student's behaviors, leading to their being addressed in the IEP inadequately or not at all.' [Caselaw cite omitted.] Indeed, that is the case here, as this failure resulted in the omission of 'global and specific hypotheses as to why [K.T.'s] problem behavior[s] occur[red],' which are minimum requirements under the law. [Legal cite omitted.] In other words, the CSE, in formulating K.T.'s IEPs, developed BIPs without the results of an FBA, and thus never attempted to address the root causes of K.T.'s interfering behaviors, thereby casting doubt on the adequacy of its provisions for treating them."

"[E]ach IEP provided K.T. with insufficiently frequent weekly speech-language instruction in an inappropriate class size... no parental counseling and training was provided for in any of the IEPs, which is a violation of New York law... We also found additional isolatednhb deficiencies in the IEPs, including the omission of any annual goals or short-term objectives related to addressing K.T.'s pica..."

Further, in addition to the absence of an FBA, no BIP was developed in accordance with the terms of the March 2011 IEP and as required by law, further undermining the SRO's conclusion that K.T.'s interfering behaviors were adequately addressed in the IEP." [Legal cite omitted.]

"Moreover, no annual goals or short-term objectives were included in the March 2011 IEP related to K.T.'s physical therapy needs despite their inclusion in his IEP just three months earlier..."

"Indeed, we are left to wonder whether these persistent errors and omissions in developing K.T.'s IEPs are the result of the CSE's failure to consult the evaluative materials available to it at the time."

"There is no doubt that these procedural violations in formulating each IEP, when taken together, deprived K.T. of a FAPE for each school year. The DOE displayed a pattern of indifference to the procedural requirements of the IDEA and carelessness in formulating K.T.'s IEPs over the period of many years, repeatedly violating its obligations under the statute, which consequently resulted in the deprivation of important educational benefits to which K.T. was entitled by law."

"The District Court denied L.O. relief on the basis that the deficiencies identified in the IEPs were 'more formal than substantive.' We have explained, however, that '[t]he initial procedural inquiry in an IDEA case 'is no mere formality,' as 'adequate compliance with the procedures prescribed would in most cases assure much if not all of what Congress wished in the way of substantive content in an IEP.'" [Caselaw cite omitted.]

"Accordingly, we reverse the judgment of the District Court and remand the case for further proceedings."

"Last, we turn to the issue of relief. Under the IDEA, 'a handicapped child does not have a right to demand public education beyond the age of twenty-one.' (cites omitted.) Here, L.O. retrospectively challenges the adequacy of the public school placement K.T. attended for three years, claiming that it did not provide him with a FAPE. In doing so, however, L.O. seeks relief that would undoubtedly extend beyond K.T.'s twenty-first birthday."

"We are directed by statute that '[i]n any action brought under the IDEA, the court 'shall grant such relief as the court determines is appropriate.' [Caselaw cite omitted.] Courts retain broad discretion in fashioning an award, restrained only by the Supreme Court's directive that the relief is to be 'appropriate' in light of the purpose of the Act.' [Caselaw cite omitted.] The Supreme Court has held that 'equitable considerations are relevant in fashioning relief in any IDEA action.' See *Burlington*, 471 U.S. at 374; see also *Doe*, 790 F.3d at 454. Further, although '[a]n award of damages is not available, . . . a court may award various forms of retroactive and prospective equitable relief, including reimbursement of tuition, compensatory education, and other declaratory and injunctive remedies.'" (cites omitted.)

"The parties contest what relief, if any, is available to L.O. under the unusual circumstances of this case. Neither the District Court nor either administrative officer, however, reached this question below. Accordingly, on remand, the District Court is directed to consider, in the first instance, what, if any, relief L.O. is entitled to as an award for K.T.'s FAPE deprivations for the 2009-2010, 2010-2011, and 2011-2012 school years. In doing so, '[w]e leave the mechanics of structuring the compensatory education award to the [D]istrict [C]ourt's sound equitable discretion, although the court may wish to consult remedies that we have endorsed in the past.'"

COPAA filed an Amicus brief with the Court in this case.

(Parent's attorneys - Philip B. Abramowitz and Andrew K. Cuddy // School's attorney - Amanda Sue Nichols)

Outcome: After losing at all earlier levels, the parents prevailed.[197]

Smith + Munoz v.
Los Angeles Unif. Sch. Dist.
822 F.3d 1065 (9th Cir. 2016)
California - 5/20/2016

The case is related to the right of individuals to intervene in renegotiated settlement orders based on class action litigation.

In 1996 in the *Chandra Smith v. LAUSD* case there was a consent decree related to Least Restrictive Environment which closed and restructured special education centers. The consent decree was modified in 2003 and more modifications considered in 2006 with an increasing number of children being placed in general education settings.

This case alleged that because of the changes in the *Chandra Smith* Decree, "severely disabled children" were being placed in general education settings and coming home with "bruises and other injuries [and] . . . 8 of the 18 special education centers [were] closed to enrollment."

"Parents were . . . not consulted in the development of their child's IEP. Rather, they are told that placement in a special education center is no longer an option."

Two sets of parents filed a lawsuit to intervene.

The Ninth Circuit explained that:

"Appellants are a sub-class of moderately to severely disabled children who have moved to intervene in a class action brought on behalf of all disabled students in the Los Angeles Unified School District ("LAUSD") against LAUSD ("the *Chanda Smith* Litigation"). Appellants seek to intervene to challenge the legality of a new policy, adopted by LAUSD in 2012 as part of a renegotiation of the *Chanda Smith* parties' settlement. That settlement requires a class of LAUSD's most severely disabled students to go to the same schools as the district's general, non-disabled student body. LAUSD calls this 'integration'; Appellants want their children to be schooled separately."

"A district court denied Appellants' motion to intervene. We conclude that the district court abused its discretion in denying Appellants' motion as untimely, and further erred when it found intervention unnecessary to protect Appellants' interest in ensuring the receipt of public education consistent with their disabilities and federal law."

The Ninth Circuit found that intervention was appropriate and reversed and remanded the case to the District Court.

(Parent's attorney - David Ward German // School's attorney - Barrett Green)

Outcome: Parents prevailed.

Timothy O v. Paso Robles Unif. Sch. Dist.
822 F.3d 1105 (9th Cir. 2016)
California - 5/23/2016

This **2016 Case of the Year** is about the assessment requirements for determining if a child with autism is qualified for an IEP.

[197] **Update**: The equitable relief extended for two years beyond the child's 22nd birthday and he is now at the Woods residential school in Pennsylvania and is reportedly is making great progress.

Luke has autism and his "parents filed a request for a due process hearing with the Office of Administrative Hearings, alleging in relevant part that Paso Robles violated the procedural and substantive requirements of the IDEA and the California Education Code by (1) failing to assess Luke in all areas of suspected disability, specifically autism; and (2) failing to appropriately address his behavioral issues, such as refusing to speak, tantrums, and non-compliance, during the 2010-2011 school year."

"They further alleged that, by violating these requirements, the school denied Luke a free appropriate public education during the 2009-2010 and 2010-2011 school years. They requested, as a remedy for these violations, that Paso Robles pay for the private assessments and private behavioral services that Luke received, that it provide Luke with compensatory behavioral and speech services, and that it include the behavioral therapy recommended by Dr. Freeman as part of Luke's ongoing educational program. His parents also withdrew Luke from school in a letter dated July 15, 2011."

"A multi-day hearing was held in March and April of 2012. On July 6, 2012, the administrative law judge (ALJ) denied all of Luke's claims... Luke's parents appealed the ALJ's decision to the United States District Court for the Central District of California. The district court affirmed the ALJ's decision, but adopted a different rationale."

The Ninth Circuit began its decision with a description of autism and the importance of intensive early intervention: "The Center for Disease Control and Prevention estimates that nearly one in sixty-eight children has autism spectrum disorder, a neurodevelopmental disorder that is characterized, in varying degrees, by difficulty communicating and socializing and by restricted repetitive behavior, interests, and activities. The disorder is present from birth, or very early in development, and affects children's ability to communicate ideas and feelings, to use their imagination, and to develop relationships with others. Every individual with autism spectrum disorder is unique, although the main characteristics in children—behavioral deficits in eye contact, responding to one's name, joint attention behavior, pretend play, imitation, nonverbal communication, and language development—are measurable by eighteen months of age."

"Early diagnosis and intervention is critical for the education of children with autism. In fact, with early and appropriate intervention, as many as 25% of children with early autism will, at an early age, no longer meet the criteria for that disorder... Indeed, the success of early intervention techniques has lowered the number of autistic children who will remain non-verbal throughout their lifetime to fewer than 10%, down from roughly 50% in the 1980s. Early intervention also minimizes the secondary symptoms and disruptive behavior, such as aggression, tantrums, and self-injury, that are displayed by children with the disorder. If left untreated, however, symptoms of autism spectrum disorder can become more severe and require extensive and expensive therapeutic interventions."

"Luke is a child with autism. Under . . . IDEA, . . . Paso Robles Unified School District (Paso Robles) became responsible for providing Luke with a free appropriate public education (FAPE) when he turned three years old . . . to ensure that children with disabilities receive an appropriate education tailored to their unique condition, the IDEA requires that when a school district is afforded reason to suspect that a child has a disability, it 'conduct a full and individual initial evaluation' that ensures the child is assessed for 'all areas of suspected disability,' using a variety of reliable and technically sound instruments." [Legal cite omitted.]

"Under the IDEA, the school district had an affirmative obligation to formally assess Luke for autism using reliable, standardized, and statutorily proscribed methods. Paso Robles, however, ignored the clear evidence requiring it to do so, and instead determined that Luke was not autistic based on the view of a staff member who opined, after a casual observation, that Luke did not display signs of autism. This failure to formally assess Luke's disability rendered the provision of a free appropriate education impossible and left his autism untreated for years while Paso Robles's staff, because of a lack of adequate information, took actions that may have been counter-productive and reinforced Luke's refusal to speak."

"We hold, therefore, that Paso Robles violated the IDEA and denied Luke a free appropriate public education during the 2009-2010 and 2010-2011 school years . . . and remand for the determination of an appropriate remedy."

COPAA filed an Amicus brief with the Court in this case.

(Parent's attorney - Marcy J.K. Tiffany[198] // School's attorney - Diane Beall)

Outcome: Parents prevailed. School district has filed a Petition for Certiorari with SCOTUS.

WR v. Ohio Dept. Health
6th Cir. 2016
Ohio - 6/10/2016

In this *Fry* exhaustion, early intervention case, the parents filed suit against the State of Ohio Department of Health (ODH) and Ohio's IDEA Part C Coordinator alleging that the "Defendants predetermined they would not provide autistic children in Ohio with the early intervention service of applied behavior analysis therapy or compensatory services and reimbursement for these services, systematically violating Part C of the IDEA and other laws."

The parents did not request a special education due process hearing, i.e., exhaust their administrative remedies. [See SCOTUS *Fry*.]

The Part C procedural safeguards statute at 20 U.S.C. § 1439(a)(1) does not specifically address "exhaustion." The statute notes that "Any party aggrieved by the findings and decision regarding an administrative complaint shall have the right to bring a civil action with respect to the complaint in any . . . district court of the United States without regard to the amount in controversy . . .the court shall receive the records of the administrative proceedings, shall hear additional evidence at the request of a party, and, basing its decision on the preponderance of the evidence, shall grant such relief as the court determines is appropriate."

The Court of Appeals explained that "A party cannot be 'aggrieved by the findings and decision regarding an administrative complaint' if they have not first participated in an administrative proceeding." The Court also noted that exhaustion is mandated in the Part C federal regulations at 34 C.F.R. § 303.448.

Relying on their own Sixth Circuit *Fry* case, an opinion this Court of Appeals issued a year prior, which was pending before the U. S. Supreme Court at the time of this case, the Court added "Because all of Plaintiffs' claims stem from the alleged IDEA violations, they are subject to the exhaustion requirements of the IDEA. Accordingly, dismissal is proper where, as here, a plaintiff has failed to exhaust administrative remedies under the IDEA. See, e.g., *Fry*, 788 F.3d at 631; S.E., 544 F.3d at 643."

Outcome: Dept of Health prevailed.

[198] On the Wrightslaw website, google the name "Tiffany" and you will see several articles she has co-authored about settlement agreements and the Atlanta GA *Draper* case.

AL v. Jackson County Sch. Bd
11th Cir. 2016
Florida - 6/13/2016

Plaintiff appealed the District Court's Order imposing sanctions for filing a frivolous lawsuit pursuant to Rule 11 of the Federal Rules of Civil Procedure. AL v. Jackson County Sch. Bd.

While a due process hearing was pending "A.L. and P.L.B. filed a complaint in district court against Jackson [and] . . . raised claims for (1) injunctive relief under the IDEA and Section 504, (2) declaratory relief based on the First Amendment, (3) denial of FAPE, (4) Section 504 discrimination, and (5) retaliation under the IDEA and Section 504. The district court dismissed all of these claims because it found that A.L. and P.L.B. failed to exhaust their administrative remedies." [See SCOTUS *Fry.*]

"A.L. and P.L.B. sought an injunction in an effort to obtain allegedly critical educational services for A.L. while an ALJ considered the merits of their IDEA and related claims. [T]he basis for this claim . . . arose during the pendency of IDEA proceedings, this claim did not present a question as to whether Jackson denied A.L. FAPE while the stay-put provision was in effect."

"The ALJ ruled on the [injunction] request in its June 2012 order and the order explicitly stated that the proper forum for A.L. and P.L.B. to pursue injunctive relief was civil court."

After the dismissal for failure to exhaust, "Jackson moved for Rule 11 sanctions [and] . . . the court concluded that A.L.'s and P.L.B.'s counsel knowingly filed a legally frivolous complaint on their behalf, thus warranting sanctions."

"We review a district court's award of Rule 11 sanctions for abuse of discretion. 'A district court ruling based on an erroneous interpretation of the law or a clearly erroneous reading of the evidence would constitute an abuse of discretion.' (cites omitted)"

"However, the purpose of Rule 11 is to deter frivolous lawsuits and not to deter novel legal arguments or cases of first impression. The dismissal of an action, 'in and of itself, does not mean that an action is frivolous or warrants the imposition of sanctions.'"

"After thorough review of the parties' briefs and the record, we conclude that the district court abused its discretion in granting Jackson's motion for sanctions. We vacate and remand."

Outcome: Sanctions vacated. Parent and attorney prevailed.

Binno v. American Bar Assoc.
826 F.3d 338 (6th Cir. 2016)
Michigan - 6/16/2016

This is an ADA discrimination case brought against the American Bar Association. The Court of Appeals summarized the facts and the legal issue in its opening paragraph.

"Plaintiff Angelo Binno is a legally blind individual who applied for admission to several law schools, unsuccessfully, and thereafter filed an action against the American Bar Association (ABA), under the Americans with Disabilities Act (ADA), claiming that his lack of success was due to a discriminatory admissions test 'mandated' by the ABA. The admissions examination in question, utilized by nearly all law schools in the United States, is the Law School Admissions Test (LSAT)."

"Binno contends that the questions on the LSAT have a discriminatory effect on the blind and visually impaired because a quarter of those questions 'require spatial reasoning and visual diagramming for successful completion.' He alleges that his poor performance on the LSAT prevented him from being admitted to accredited law schools, in violation of Titles III and V of the ADA."

"The district court granted the ABA's motion to dismiss, finding that plaintiff Binno lacked standing to sue the ABA and, alternatively, that his amended complaint failed to state a claim for relief under either Title III or Title V of the ADA as a matter of law."

"We affirm, concluding that Binno does not have standing to sue the ABA because his injury was not caused by the ABA and because it is unlikely that his injury would be redressed by a favorable decision against the ABA. Moreover, even if Binno could establish standing, the district court correctly dismissed his Title III and Title V claims for failure to state claims for which relief may be granted."

"The ABA responds that . . . the LSAT is written, administered, and scored by the Law School Admission Council (LSAC), an entity that is not part of the ABA. The LSAC provides accommodations for persons with disabilities who wish to take the LSAT. These accommodations include, but are not limited to, additional time to complete the test and the use of a reader during the examination."

"In its explanation, the Court noted that: '[T]he ABA argues that because it is neither responsible for the content of the LSAT nor for law schools' use of the LSAT in law school admissions, Binno's injury is not caused by the ABA's actions. In that sense, the district court correctly noted that Binno sued the wrong party. The law schools to which he applied, not the ABA, determine what weight, if any, to give Binno's LSAT score, and the entity in control of the LSAT's content and format is not the ABA but the LSAC."

"For the reasons set out above, we affirm the judgment of the district court. In doing so, however, we are left puzzled by Binno's failure to litigate against the LSAC, rather than the ABA."

(Plaintiff's attorney - Jason Marc Turkish // Attorney for ABA - Anne E. Rea)

Outcome: American Bar Assoc. prevailed.

Ramona Smith v. Cheyenne Mountain Sch. Dist. 12
10th Cir. 2016
Colorado - 6/16/2016

This is a stay put case in which the parent wanted the stay put placement to be a private school even though the child had not attended the private school.

The Court discussed the various legal definitions of the term "educational placement" and noted that the child was not actually attending "CMCA at the time of the hearing on the stay-put motion, the IEP in place at that time was the May 2014 IEP, which listed CMCA as his school of attendance. In addition, R.S. had attended CMCA the previous school year for kindergarten. Although Ms. Smith contends that R.S. is entitled to a proper placement at an unidentified private school, transferring him to a new school (without any showing that the new school could implement the IEP) would not comply with the stay-put provision. We conclude that R.S.'s stay-put placement was CMCA. Consequently, the School District is not required to fund a private-school placement for R.S."

Outcome: School district prevailed.

Baquerizo v. Garden Grove Unif. Sch. Dist.
826 F.3d 1179 (2016)
California - 6/22/2016

This tuition reimbursement case is convoluted, with several due process hearings, appeals to federal court and settlement agreements.

"[U]until he graduated from high school in 2014, Carlos, his Guardian, and Garden Grove have litigated the issue of whether Garden Grove is required to reimburse Guardian for Carlos's private instruction with regard to every school year since 2007."

In this case, which is on appeal from District Court, the child's "Guardian waited almost two years to challenge the June 2009 IEP and request reimbursement. On June 15, 2011, she filed a request for a due process hearing. During the intervening two years, the parties held an IEP for the 2010-2011 school year and initiated administrative proceedings over that IEP. Because of the delay, the dispute over the 2009-2010 school year was consolidated with the litigation over the 2011-2012 school year."

The Ninth Circuit explained that reimbursement is sought ". . . for the cost of Carlos's private education during the 2009-2010 and 2011-2012 school years. . . The administrative law judge (ALJ) denied reimbursement, and the district court affirmed."

In describing the earlier litigation, the Court noted that "The Garrett[199] Decision addressed the 13 months immediately prior to the June 2009 IEP, and ruled that up until June 17, 2009, Guardian had thwarted Garden Grove's 'great efforts to conduct assessments' by being uncooperative. The First *Selna* Decision upheld the *Garrett* Decision in its entirety, and was not appealed. In this appeal, Guardian suggests that the previous litigation—centered around Garden Grove's failure to conduct assessments through June 17, 2009—should have no bearing on whether the goals set one day later were supported by appropriate assessments. Not so. The ability of Garden Grove to obtain assessments prior to the meeting on June 18, and arrive armed with that data, is directly relevant to whether any procedural defects were excusable. Thus, the *Garrett*

[199] Garrett was the Administrative Law Judge.

Decision precludes Guardian from arguing that Garden Grove violated the IDEA because it failed to assess Carlos in time for the June 2009 IEP."

"We agree with the district court and ALJ Ruff that any procedural failure on the part of Garden Grove was caused by Guardian, and that, in any event, the Jordan Intermediate School placement was a FAPE."

With regard to the June 2009 IEP, the Court held "We agree with ALJ Ruff and with the district court that any procedural violation of the IDEA on the part of Garden Grove is excused because they were directly caused by Guardian."

As to the June 2011 IEP, the Court stated: "Before the ALJ, Guardian presented a laundry list of violations . . . ALJ Ruff carefully walked through each alleged violation, and concluded that none was meritorious. On appeal, Guardian only asserts two arguments: that Garden Grove failed to assess Carlos for anxiety, and that '[n]o baselines were determined' for Carlos's speech and language goals."

"By Guardian's own admission at the IEP meeting, an assessment of Carlos's anxiety would not have significantly changed the educational plan in the IEP, because Carlos's anxiety was being effectively managed by medication and breathing exercises."

"As to Carlos's speech and language goals, the contention before the agency (toward which Guardian only gestures in her brief on appeal) was that Garden Grove did not have enough specific information to create a baseline for Carlos in order to build an appropriate goal. . . ALJ Ruff concluded that 'under these highly unusual circumstances in which a pupil was kept out of a classroom environment for approximately four years,' the school district created an IEP plan that was as concrete as possible with the available data."

The Court of Appeals explained that "Because Garden Grove did not violate the IDEA in either the June 2009 IEP or June 2011 IEP, the judgment of the district court is affirmed [and tuition reimbursement is denied]."

(Parent's attorney - Tania L. Whiteleather // School's attorney - S. Daniel Harbottle)

Outcome: School prevailed.

Moore v. Kansas City Sch.
828 F. 3d 687 (8th Cir. 2016)
Missouri - 7/7/2016

This rape case contains legal issues related to removal of state cases to federal court, whether there was a "federal question" and, because the child had an IEP, the SCOTUS *Fry* issues of failure to exhaust administrative remedies.

"On behalf of D.S., a minor student with intellectual disabilities, Katie Moore sued Kansas City Public Schools (school district), Southwest Early College Campus (Southwest), the superintendent of the school district, the principal of Southwest, a special education teacher, and a para-professional at Southwest (collectively, defendants) in Missouri state court."

"The petition did not request any change or amendment to D.S.'s IEP or educational placement, and the state law claims do not rely on the IDEA or the rights it creates and protects."

"The petition sought damages for premises liability and negligent supervision because D.S. was raped by another student in an unsupervised area of Southwest during the school day, and because D.S. was repeatedly bullied and sexually harassed by her classmates and peers."

"The school district and Southwest removed the lawsuit to the Western District of Missouri . . . claiming Moore's causes of action arose under the Individuals with Disabilities Education Act, and then moved to dismiss under Federal Rule of Civil Procedure 12(b)(1) and (6). The district court denied Moore's motion to remand and then dismissed the lawsuit for failure to exhaust IDEA administrative remedies." The parents appealed the removal from state court and subsequent dismissal of their case for their failure to exhaust administrative remedies.

"D.S. was a special education student at Southwest during the 2013-14 school year. Due to her intellectual and learning disabilities at the time relevant to the complaint, D.S. sometimes had trouble communicating and spoke in 'baby talk.' D.S. also had difficulty perceiving danger and was 'susceptible to suggestion due to her significant intellectual and learning disabilities'. . .To accommodate her disability, D.S. had an individualized education program (IEP)."

"At school, D.S. was relentlessly bullied and harassed by her peers."

"On April 1, 2014, around 10:44 a.m., a para-professional assigned to D.S.'s classroom watched D.S. leave the lunchroom and enter a hallway before the end of the period. Sometime between then and 2 p.m. that day, two students led D.S. through a set of unsecured doors, where a male student raped her while another female student acted as a 'look-out.' . . . Around 2:00 a.m. the next morning, D.S. told her parents she was experiencing vaginal and anal pain. D.S. was taken to Children's Mercy Hospital, where it was confirmed D.S. had been vaginally and anally raped."

"The gravamen of the petition is a state law action for damages seeking redress for the brutal injuries D.S. suffered as the result of repeated sexual assault and rape while under Southwest's supervision."

"The defendants failed to satisfy their burden of establishing federal jurisdiction. We reverse the district court's judgment with instructions to remand this case to the Missouri state court from which the action was removed."

(Parent's attorney - Edward D. Robertson, Jr. // School's attorney - Tyson H. Ketchum)

Outcome: Case reinstated, not dismissed, remanded to state court. Parents prevailed.

Spring v. Allegany-Limestone Cent. Sch. Dist.
2nd Cir. 2016
Per Curium
New York - 7/14/2016

Keri Spring filed suit[200] alleging that her son, Gregory Spring's suicide, was the result of his "severe emotional distress, humiliation, embarrassment, and self-loathing" was caused by the defendants' "acts and omissions, including negligence, gross negligence, recklessness and/or deliberate indifference to disabilities, bullying, and discriminatory conduct."

The suit was based on 504 / ADA, Constitutional, and New York state civil rights claims.

The District Court dismissed the case in its entirety explaining that the federal court complaint ". . . fails to sufficiently allege that any Plaintiff engaged in protected activity under the ADA or Rehabilitation Act. Although there are numerous general allegations that Plaintiff Keri Spring complained of bullying and the lack of an anti-bullying policy, Plaintiffs do not allege that Keri complained that the bullying was on account of Gregory's purported disability. . . (complaints of 'bullying,' without more, are insufficient to establish protected activity under the ADA or Section 504). Plaintiffs do allege that Keri Spring complained to Defendant Straub on six different occasions between January and June 2013 about 'Defendant Easton and his behavior,' which was previously alleged to include 'mocking and mimicking [Gregory's] disability related tics.'"[201]

The Court of Appeals upheld the dismissal of most claims explaining that "[w]e affirm the District Court's dismissal of Plaintiffs' complaint failed to allege adequately that Gregory's named conditions substantially limited him in a major life activity and further determined that the proposed amendments to the complaint failed to cure this defect."

"[T]he District Court clearly misconstrued the amended pleadings and misapplied the law."

"The proposed second amended complaint explicitly identified the effects of Gregory's conditions on his major life activities of, inter alia, 'speaking,' 'learning,' 'concentrating,' and 'communicating,' identifying 'a long-standing record of suffering with a variety of motor and vocal tics' with a specific list of examples including 'outbursts,' 'involuntary knee slapping and eye blinking tics,' 'repetitive utterance of foul language,' and 'repetitive questioning.' It further alleged that the effects intensified 'during periods of stress or unfamiliar settings or situations' and that his disabilities 'substantially limited his ability to communicate' because 'he was unable to recognize

---

[200] The Complaint is at: http://www.wrightslaw.com/law/pleadings/2016.0831.complaint.ny.suicide.spring.allegany.amended.pdf

[201] **Wrightslaw note**: The Court of Appeals Opinion does not provide the facts of the case, thus the source for the preceding paragraphs was the U. S. District Court decision issued on September 30, 2015, published in 138 F.Supp.3d 282, W.D.NY.

emotions communicated by tone of voice and misunderstanding of social cues.'"

"Taken together, the proposed amendments substantive due process claims . . . equal protection claims . . . claim of disparate treatment [and] deliberate indifference . . . retaliation claims, *Monell* liability claims . . . state constitutional claims [and] state statutory and common-law claims."

"The District Court dismissed Plaintiffs' ADA and Rehabilitation Act claims on the ground that the alleged sufficient facts to make plausible that the impact on Gregory's learning ability, which also prompted a need for special education services, constituted a substantial limitation. On the facts alleged, therefore, we conclude that these proposed amendments would have sufficed to meet the requirements of a qualifying disability, particularly given the ADA Amendments Act of 2008's significant relaxation of the standard for substantial limits on major life activities."

"Accordingly, we vacate the District Court's denial of leave to amend and so much of the judgment as dismissed Plaintiffs' ADA and Rehabilitation Act claims."

"The case is REMANDED for further proceedings consistent with this order."

(Plaintiff's attorney - A.J. Bosman // School's attorney - Jenna W. Klucsik)

Outcome: Parent prevailed on Section 504 and ADA claims; others were dismissed.[202] [203]

Ms. S v. Regional Sch. Unit 72
829 F.3d 95, 1st Cir. 2016
Maine - 7/15/2016

This is a tuition reimbursement and statute of limitations (SOL) case [which] "concerns two separate, but ultimately intertwining, narratives. The first is that of appellant, Ms. S., her son, B.S., and his right to a free appropriate public education (FAPE) under the federal Individuals with Disabilities Education Act (IDEA). The second concerns the implementation of a Maine regulation - referred to herein as the 'filing limitation' - that determines how much time a parent, such as Ms. S., has to request a due process hearing alleging an IDEA violation."

"In May 2013, Ms. S. filed a request for a due process hearing with the Maine Department of Education (MDOE) concerning alleged IDEA violations in all of B.S.'s ninth (2009-2010), tenth (2010-2011), eleventh (2011-2012), and twelfth (2012-2013) grade years. The hearing officer dismissed the claims that arose during B.S.'s ninth and tenth grades as time barred because the filing limitation allowed only claims brought within two years of when the parent knew or should have known of a violation."

"Ms. S. sought judicial review in the district court, arguing that the hearing officer should not have dismissed the ninth and tenth grade claims because the two-year filing limitation was not promulgated in compliance with the Maine Administrative Procedure Act (Maine APA or MAPA) and is therefore void and of no legal effect. The district court determined that the two-year filing limitation was valid, Ms. S. did not qualify for an exception to the limitation period, and B.S. received a FAPE in the eleventh and twelfth grades. Ms. S.'s timely appeal followed."

"We conclude that the district court erred in its analysis of the validity of the two-year filing limitation, and, further, that the record before us is insufficient to determine whether the MDOE adequately complied with MAPA procedures when adopting the two-year filing limitation. Given that conclusion, we do not reach the question of whether an exception to the filing limitation applies here. However, we do find that, consistent with the district court's judgment, B.S. received a FAPE in the eleventh and twelfth grades. We therefore vacate and remand in part, and affirm in part."

"[W]e vacate the district court's judgment that the two-year filing limitation is valid under the Maine APA and remand to the district court for

---

[202] **Update**: This case returned to the District Court on August 4, 2016. The Plaintiffs filed a new Amended Complaint on August 31, 2016. This was followed by a series of Motions, Cross Motions, Affidavits and Memorandum. The last document filed was an Affidavit on October 28, 2016. Nothing else is on file with the U. S. District Court.

[203] At press time, Counsel for Plaintiff advised that the parties are awaiting a ruling from the Judge on the outstanding pleadings. Future updates, when known, will be available on our Federal Courts Complaint page at: http://www.wrightslaw.com/law/pleadings/fed.court.complaints.htm

further proceedings consistent with this opinion. We affirm the district court's judgment that B.S. received a FAPE in the eleventh and twelfth grades."

(Parent's attorney - Richard O'Meara)

Outcome: Parents partially prevailed on S/L issue. School district prevailed on tuition reimbursement for two years.

Gibson v. Forest Hills Sch. Dist.
6th Cir. 2016
Ohio - 7/15/2016

In this transition, attorney fee case, "The district court held that Forest Hills denied Chloe a FAPE by failing to adequately plan for her postsecondary future." The parents sought over $800,000 in attorneys' fees. The District Court only awarded $327,641. Both parties appealed to the Sixth Circuit.

Judge Boggs wrote that "Chloe's disability and seizure disorder have left her with an IQ of between forty-three and fifty-seven, and have given her difficulty with simple math and reasoning tasks, such as counting and telling time. Despite these setbacks, Chloe has learned to read at a third-grade level, and has also shown an ability to learn basic routines and complete repetitive tasks, such as bussing tables and unpacking boxes. In short, although Chloe's disability poses challenges for her daily life, she has made significant progress in overcoming them."

"In particular, the district court found that Forest Hills never invited Chloe to transition-related meetings, in violation of federal and Ohio regulations. The court found that Forest Hills compounded this error by failing to take other steps to consider Chloe's transition-related preferences and interests, as required by 34 C.F.R. § 300.321(b)(2) and Ohio Admin. Code 3301-51-07(I)(2)(b). The court also found that until Goodwill Industries conducted its vocational assessment, at which time Chloe was nineteen years old, Forest Hills had failed to conduct any age-appropriate assessments related to Chloe's transition into adult life. The court concluded that without information about Chloe's preferences, interests, or abilities, Forest Hills could not properly plan for Chloe's transition and therefore denied her a FAPE."

"The district court held that Forest Hills denied Chloe a FAPE by violating three of the IDEA's procedural requirements. As we explain, we agree."

"The district court held that Forest Hills violated the IDEA's procedural requirements in three ways: by failing to invite Chloe to participate in IEP Team meetings, failing to take other meaningful steps to ensure that her transition-related interests were considered, and failing to conduct any age-appropriate transition assessments."

"Chloe's progress at Forest Hills does not negate the possibility that adherence to IDEA procedures would have enabled Forest Hills to design a work-oriented educational plan that would have allowed Chloe to be more self-sufficient than she was at the time of the due process complaint. For this reason, we agree with the district court that Forest Hills denied Chloe a FAPE."

"Having resolved Forest Hills's appeals in the Gibsons' favor, we turn to the Gibsons' appeal of the district court's fee awards. We review a district court's decision to award attorney's fees in an IDEA case for abuse of discretion, using the principles established for fee awards in federal civil-rights actions."

"The Gibsons initially moved for attorney's fees in the amount of $800,314.50, a figure they compiled by taking the product of the hourly rates of each of their attorneys and paralegals and the number of hours that each attorney and paralegal worked. The district court undertook a lodestar calculation using average hourly rates of attorneys and paralegals in the Southern District of Ohio and found that the Gibsons' request of $800,314.50 approximated the resulting lodestar value."

"But after mentioning various considerations, including its finding that both the Gibsons and Forest Hills had contributed to the 'protracted nature of this litigation,' the district court ultimately decided to reduce the Gibsons' fee award by 62.5% to $300,000 on the ground that the 'success achieved by the Gibsons was limited in proportion to the total relief requested.'"

". . . Forest Hills failed to comply with the IDEA's procedural requirements, and that these procedural violations ultimately denied Chloe a FAPE. But because the district court did not adequately explain the reasons for departing from its lodestar calculation, we must vacate the court's fee awards and remand those awards for further consideration."

The Court affirmed the finding that Forest Hills violated IDEA and remanded the case back for a recalculation of the attorneys' fee award.

COPAA filed an Amicus brief with the Court in this case.

Outcome: Parents prevailed. Case remanded for recalculation of attorneys' fees.

AM v. Holmes
830 F.3d 1123 (10th Cir. 2016)
New Mexico - 7/25/2016
[Dissent by new SCOTUS Justice Gorsuch]

[**Wrightslaw note** - This case is **not** related to IDEA, 504, or ADA. This is a school arrest, violation of Constitutional rights case.[204] The dissent was written by Neil Gorsuch, newest Justice on the Supreme Court, and is included for that reason.]

A.M., on behalf of her thirteen-year-old child, F.M., filed suit against the building principal, assistant principal, and Albuquerque Police Officer, Arthur Acosta.

"[The complaint alleged] that the defendants deprived F.M. of his civil rights by arresting him . . . and handcuffing him" in violation of the Fourth Amendment. "A reasonable officer 'should have known that burping was not a crime' and that 'no force was necessary' to facilitate the arrest [and that] . . . Ms. LaBarge's 'strip-searching' of F.M. was unreasonable" [and in violation of the Fourth Amendment.]

The district court dismissed the case. The parent appealed to the Tenth Circuit. That Court, by a 2 to 1 vote, upheld the dismissal. Judge Gorsuch did not agree.

The opinion, including 24 footnotes, is 94 pages long. Of interest is the dissent by Judge Gorsuch. A portion of his dissent is reproduced below.

"If a seventh grader starts trading fake burps for laughs in gym class, what's a teacher to do? Order extra laps? Detention? A trip to the principal's office? Maybe. But then again, maybe that's too old school. Maybe today you call a police officer. And maybe today, the officer decides that, instead of just escorting the now compliant thirteen-year old to the principal's office, an arrest would be a better idea. So out come the handcuffs and off goes the child to juvenile detention. My colleagues suggest the law permits exactly this option and they offer ninety-four pages explaining why they think that's so. Respectfully, I remain unpersuaded."

"My colleagues likewise dismiss the authority from other states interpreting similar statutes similarly. But again, it's hard to see why. After all, these cases draw the same distinction suggested by Silva — between childish pranks and more seriously disruptive behaviors — and hold that only the latter are prohibited by statutes like the one before us today. And they draw that distinction, too, because disciplining children who temporarily distract classmates and interrupt lessons 'is simply part of [traditional] school activity' and part of its 'lawful mission ... or function.' Given that, I would have thought these cases would have only reinforced the lesson Silva already taught reasonable officers in New Mexico." [Caselaw cite omitted.]

"Often enough the law can be 'an ass — an idiot,' Charles Dickens, *Oliver Twist* 520 (Dodd, Mead & Co. 1941) (1838) — and there is little we judges can do about it, for it is (or should be) emphatically our job to apply, not rewrite, the law enacted by the people's representatives. Indeed, a judge who likes every result he reaches is very likely a bad judge, reaching for results he prefers rather than those the law compels. So it is I admire my colleagues today, for no doubt they reach a result they dislike but believe the law demands — and in that I see the best of our profession and much to admire. It's only that, in this case, I don't believe the law happens to be quite as much of an ass as they do. I respectfully dissent."

(Parent's attorney - Joseph P. Kennedy // School's attorney - Emil J. Kiehne)

Outcome: School prevailed. Parent's suit for violation of civil rights dismissed over Judge Gorsuch's objections.

---

[204] Compare this case to the 2/19/2017 Tenth Circuit's *JV v. Albuquerque Pub. Sch.* which involved handcuffing a seven-year-old student who kicked and shot rubber bands at a school security officer. The child had an IEP and BIP and was unsuccessful alleging violations of Section 504 and ADA.

MM v. NYC DOE
2nd Cir. 2016
New York - 7/26/2016

In this New York tuition reimbursement case, the District Court upheld the decision of the Reviewing Officer who ruled in favor of the school district.

On appeal to the Second Circuit, the parent asserted that the school district failed "(1) to specify in J.S.'s IEP the mandated frequency, location, and duration of J.S.'s transition services . . . and (2) to conduct a mandated triennial evaluation of J.S., including required vocational and transition assessments. These procedural defects, M.M. contends, denied J.S.'s right to a FAPE." The Second Circuit did not agree.

"Procedural violations result in the denial of a FAPE only 'if they [1] 'impeded the child's right to a [FAPE],' [2] 'significantly impeded the parents' opportunity to participate in the decision-making process,' or [3] 'caused a deprivation of educational benefits.'"

"Multiple procedural violations may cumulatively result in the denial of a FAPE even if the violations considered individually do not."

"While the SRO did not specifically address in his March 18, 2014 decision the application of the IDEA's 'frequency, location, and duration' requirement to J.S.'s recommended transitional and vocational services . . . the SRO discussed the IEP's provision for those services at length. The SRO thoroughly and carefully reviewed the IEP's transitional and vocational components, properly using testimony to explain how these services would be implemented."

"As to M.M.'s second argument, we agree that the DOE should have performed a reevaluation of J.S. at least once within the three years preceding the May 22, 2012 IEP meeting. . . Nevertheless, '[a]lthough the applicable statutory provision does mandate the DOE to conduct a triennial reevaluation of a student at least every three years, the lack of such a reevaluation in this case did not render the IEP inappropriate.' The SRO, after 'thorough and careful' review of the record, determined that the committee that had developed J.S.'s IEP had before it 'sufficient evaluative information,' The committee had before it three reports concerning J.S. In addition, the committee 'considered input' from M.M. and two teachers affiliated with the school in which J.S. was enrolled at the time, including his 'then-current English language arts teacher.' According the SRO's opinion 'due weight,' we conclude that the DOE's procedural violation did not deny J.S. a FAPE."

"We have considered M.M.'s remaining arguments and find them to be without merit. Accordingly, we AFFIRM the judgment of the district court."

COPAA filed an Amicus brief with the Court in this case.

(Parent's attorney - Erin McCormack-Herbert // School's attorney - Diana Lawless)

Outcome: School district prevailed.

Doe v. Cape Elizabeth Sch. Dist.
832 F.3d 69 (1st Cir. 2016)
Maine - 8/5/2016

In this LD eligibility case, the First Circuit explained, "We are asked, in essence, to decide whether a child with a strong academic record may still be found to have a learning disability and a need for special education, thereby entitling her to special education and related services."

"Appellants Mr. and Mrs. Doe ('the Does') appeal the decision of the district court, which affirmed the administrative hearing officer's determination that their child, Jane Doe ('Jane'), is no longer eligible to receive special education under the IDEA despite allegedly suffering from a reading fluency deficit. The Does argue that the district court erred as a matter of law in its eligibility inquiry because (i) the court considered Jane's overall academic achievement, when her deficiency in reading fluency is sufficient by itself to support eligibility, and (ii) the district court did not make an independent judgment as to Jane's reading fluency deficit, instead deferring to the hearing officer's factual findings, while summarily dismissing the additional evidence that the Does submitted."

"Having carefully considered the claims, we conclude that, while Jane's overall academic performance could potentially be relevant in determining whether she has a reading fluency deficit, the district court erred in relying on such evidence without regard to how it reflects her reading fluency skills. Additionally, we find that the court failed to make an independent judgment as to the additional evidence submitted by the Does and afforded excessive deference to the hearing officer's determinations in weighing the relevant reading fluency measures. Hence, we vacate and remand the case."

"We clarify, however, that even if the district court finds on remand that Jane has a reading fluency deficit, she would not be eligible for special education unless she also 'needs' special education."

COPAA filed an Amicus brief with the Court in this case.

(Parent's attorney - Richard L. O'Meara // School's attorney - Eric R. Herlan)

Outcome: Parents prevailed.[205]

SD v. Haddon Heights Bd. of Ed. 833 F. 3d 389 (3rd Cir. 2016) New Jersey - 8/18/2016

In this SCOTUS *Fry* exhaustion issue, the "plaintiffs alleged that, during Ryan's junior and senior years, the school district engaged in retaliatory acts against them, such as changing Ryan's tutor, assigning Ryan to a teacher who was known to be a bully, and refusing to allow Ryan to participate in extracurricular activities. The plaintiffs then sued, asserting three federal claims: (1) retaliation/failure to provide a FAPE, in violation of the IDEA; (2) retaliation in violation of Section 504; and (3) retaliation in violation of the ADA."

The District Court dismissed Appellants' claims pursuant to Federal Rule of Civil Procedure 12(b)(1) for lack of subject matter jurisdiction because Appellants failed to exhaust the administrative process provided for by the Individuals with Disabilities Education Act. In doing so, the District Court relied on our opinion in *Batchelor v. Rose Tree Media School District*, 759 F.3d 266 (3d Cir. 2014)[206], in which we held that claims that a school district retaliated against a child and/or the child's parents for enforcing the child's rights under the IDEA, although brought pursuant to non-IDEA statutes, were subject to the IDEA exhaustion requirement."

"The narrow question before us here is whether claims that a board of education discriminated against a student and/or the student's parents based on his disability, and retaliated against them for enforcing the child's rights under a non-IDEA statute, are subject to the IDEA exhaustion requirement. Because Appellants' alleged injuries are educational in nature and implicate services within the purview of the IDEA, we conclude that Appellants' claims must be exhausted under the IDEA."

"Although Appellants' non-IDEA claims do not . . . arise from their enforcement of rights explicitly under the IDEA, . . . we nevertheless conclude, based on the nature of Appellants' allegations, that their discrimination and retaliation claims are subject to the IDEA exhaustion requirement."

(Parent's attorney - Judith A. Gran // School's attorney - Joseph F. Betley)

Outcome: School district prevailed.[207]

Swanger v. Warrior Run Sch. Dist. 3rd Cir. 2016 Pennsylvania - 8/31/2016

In this confidentiality of records case, the victim of a sexual assault requested that the trial court review the aggressor's file, "in camera," (i.e., in private, in chambers) to determine which documents may be released to the victim's counsel. The Court refused, citing the state Mental Health Procedures Act (MHPA) which states that such documents "shall be kept confidential and, without the person's written consent, may not be released or their contents disclosed to anyone."

"In March 2011, Duane Mattison molested B.J.S., a mentally challenged young girl, as the two sat in a special education class at Warrior Run High School. Mattison had a long, troubled history of sexual

---

[205] **Update**: After remand, the case settled.

[206] See SCOTUS *Fry* which may be deemed to void this decision.

[207] **Update:** A Petition for Certiorari to SCOTUS is pending.

misconduct, both as a victim and as an aggressor, and had been undergoing treatment with Diversified Treatment Alternatives (DTA), a nonprofit organization that provides psychiatric treatment to troubled male youths. Following the assault, B.J.S.'s parents, Elaine and Victor Swanger, sued Warrior Run School District, DTA, and several individuals associated with these organizations, alleging they knew that Mattison was a sexual predator and therefore knowingly placed B.J.S. in danger, and asserting various claims under both state and federal law. The District Court granted summary judgment against the Swangers on all counts." ". . . [T]he District Court erred when it denied the Swangers' earlier motion to review in camera approximately 1,500 pages of documents from Mattison's DTA treatment file to determine which ones were privileged. We will thus vacate the District Court's order denying this motion, as well as its subsequent summary judgment orders, and remand for further proceedings consistent with this opinion."

"[T]he District Court's adoption of the MHPA kept all of the documents from view, which may have wrongfully deprived the Swangers of the opportunity to prove their case with a full record and, as we note below, runs counter to the federal policy of open disclosure." Reversed and remanded.

Outcome: Parents seeking records prevailed.

LJ v. Pittsburg Unif. Sch. Dist.
835 F.3d 1168 (9th Cir. 2016)
California - 9/1/2016

In this eligibility case, the ALJ held that a suicidal child was not eligible for an IEP. This decision was upheld by District Court. Parents appealed to the Ninth Circuit. Case reversed.

The Ninth Circuit noted that even though the "emotionally troubled young child" had "suicidal tendencies beginning in the second grade" and "attention deficit hyperactivity disorder ('ADHD') . . . [Pittsburg] "determined that L.J. was not entitled to special education services because he was not disabled."

"The district court reviewed the record and found that L.J. was disabled under three categories defined by the IDEA. It nevertheless concluded that an IEP for specialized services was not necessary because of L.J.'s satisfactory performance in general education classes. The court discounted L.J.'s suicide attempts as not bearing on the need for educational services because they took place outside of school."

"The school records show, however, that beginning in the second grade and continuing into the third and fourth grades, when the parent invoked administrative remedies, the School District had already been providing L.J. with special services, including counseling, one-on-one assistance, and instructional accommodations. These services resulted in L.J.'s materially improved performance. The School District consistently refused, however, to provide him with an IEP that would ensure such services in the future as required by the IDEA. The record also reflects that the School District violated procedural protections of the IDEA by failing to provide the parents with education records bearing on L.J.'s disabilities and services that had been provided.

"The critical issue in this appeal therefore is whether L.J. demonstrated a need for special education services. This case differs from most IDEA cases in that L.J. never received an IEP because the School District continually maintained he had no qualifying disabilities."

"The ALJ agreed that he had no qualifying disabilities. The district court held that the ALJ was incorrect in this regard and that L.J. had qualifying disabilities. The district court went on to conclude, however, that L.J. was performing satisfactorily without the need for special education services. We must therefore determine whether general education was appropriate or whether L.J. exhibited a need for special education services."

"The district court nonetheless concluded that L.J. was not eligible for special education because he was academically performing satisfactorily without receiving special education services and on the basis of the general education curriculum. This was clear error because L.J. was receiving special services, including mental health counseling and assistance from a one-on-one para educator. These are not services offered to general education students."

"The problem with the district court's analysis is that many of the services the district court viewed as general education services were in fact special education services tailored to L.J.'s situation. The district court thus classified many of the services L.J. received as general education, when they were not."

"Because L.J. is eligible for special education, the School District must formulate an IEP. We reverse the district court's decision and remand for it to order that the School District provide that remedy."

[On another note,] ". . . the School District failed to disclose assessments, treatment plans, and progress notes from L.J.'s time at Lincoln."

"In sum, the School District clearly violated important procedural safeguards set forth in the IDEA. The School District failed to disclose assessments, treatment plans, and progress notes kept by Lincoln, which deprived L.J.'s mother of her right to informed consent."

"When this matter returns to the School District for the preparation of an IEP, the School District must comply with the IDEA's procedural safeguards. Additional procedural violations can only result in the further protraction of proceedings and costly financial and emotional burdens for all those involved."

"L.J. is a child with disabilities within the meaning of the IDEA and needs special education. The judgment of the district court is reversed and the matter remanded to the district court with instruction to order the School District to provide an appropriate remedy. Reversed and remanded."

Outcome: Parents prevailed.

Gohl v. Livonia Public Sch. Dist.
836 F. 3d 672 (6th Cir. 2016)
Michigan - 9/8/2016

This case is about teacher abuse of a student. The parent alleged that his special education teacher, Sharon Turbiak "taught a preschool class that required sensitivity to mentally and physically disabled children. . . The question at hand is whether her conduct also violated the United States Constitution, two federal statutes (the Americans with Disabilities Act and the Rehabilitation Act), and Michigan law. Because Gohl did not provide sufficient evidence from which a reasonable jury could find in her favor, as the district court concluded in a thorough 39-page opinion granting summary judgment to the defendants, we affirm."

Judge Sutton, the author of the decision, joined by Judge Boggs, discussed the alleged facts of the case, the nature of the legal allegations, the basis for relief. They concluded that the parent had insufficient evidence to proceed. However, Judge Clay filed a very strong dissent and attacked their positions on both the facts and the law. For any attorney who may be preparing a Section 504 / ADA abuse by teacher case, this case and the dissent is required reading. Judge Clay's dissent provides the framework for asserting a violation of 504 / ADA.

"J.G. was born with hydrocephalus, a disorder that causes an unsafe buildup of fluid in the brain. He underwent numerous surgeries to correct or ameliorate the condition."

"During the school year, Turbiak faced several complaints about her teaching (and her relationship with her colleagues) and one complaint about her teaching of J.G."

"An occupational therapist said that Turbiak was 'gruff and abrupt'; that Turbiak once force-fed a gagging and crying student; and that Turbiak 'picked up [children] from the floor by one arm and that there was the potential to dislocate a small shoulder.'"

"Gohl filed this lawsuit on J.G.'s behalf, alleging that Livonia Public Schools, Turbiak, Respondek, Moore, and other members of the school system violated J.G.'s rights under federal and state law. The district court granted summary judgment for the defendants on Gohl's federal claims and declined to exercise supplemental jurisdiction over the state law claims."

"On appeal, Gohl claims the district court should have allowed four sets of her claims to go to a jury: (1) the substantive due process claim against Turbiak; (2) the Americans with Disabilities Act and Rehabilitation Act claims against Livonia Public Schools; (3) the equal protection claims against all defendants; and (4) all of the claims involving municipal liability for Livonia Public Schools."

"[T]he novelty of Gohl's theory of injury means that she cannot overcome Turbiak's qualified immunity. Government employees are generally shielded from civil liability unless their conduct violates a clearly established constitutional right such that a reasonable official would have known that his conduct was unlawful."

"Gohl's statutory claims fail for two reasons. She has not provided enough evidence for a reasonable jury to find that J.G. was denied participation in or a benefit of his education program, and she has failed to show that any of the challenged actions occurred 'because of' or 'solely by reason of' J.G.'s disability."

"Gohl's claims fail for another, independent reason: she cannot meet the causation requirement. Both the Americans with Disabilities Act and the Rehabilitation Act require the challenged discrimination to occur because of disability, which is another way of saying that the plaintiff must establish a but-for relationship between the protested act and the individual's disability."

"Because the record would not permit a reasonable jury to find that Livonia Public Schools excluded, denied benefits to, or discriminated against J.G. 'because of' or 'solely by reason of' his disability, Gohl's statutory claims fail as a matter of law."

"For these reasons, we affirm."

Dissent by Judge Clay - "All that matters here is that Gohl has presented enough evidence to create a genuine issue of material fact on each of her claims, and as a result, her case should go to a jury. For these reasons, this case should be reversed and remanded. I respectfully dissent."

"[T]he majority seems to be suggesting that Gohl prove a negative by adducing evidence that what happened to disabled students did not happen to students without disabilities."

"But the record clearly shows that in all the time Turbiak was abusing her disabled students, the school district received no complaints about any abuse being committed against students without disabilities; and the majority cannot seriously dispute that. Despite what the majority says, to get past summary judgment, Gohl need not adduce evidence about allegations for which there is no factual support."

"If you read only the majority opinion, you would think that this is an open and shut case. But here is what the majority downplays or leaves out completely. J.G., like several other of Sharon Turbiak's disabled students—the ones she treated 'like animals' - had a target on their backs. The things that happened to them—being force-fed while crying and gagging, being screamed at in their faces, being violently grabbed and pushed to the ground, being put in restraints made of potato chip cans, having their chairs pulled out from under them, or being otherwise humiliated and treated like something less than human—happened for the simple reason that Turbiak liked 'to target lower functioning students.' After all, Turbiak had, as she put it, 'a sick sense of humor.'"

"The majority does not tell the full story. . . J.G. has undergone several surgeries to his head, including having a retroperitoneal shunt implanted in his brain. As a result, any severe head movement could be life threatening to him. Because of the seriousness of J.G.'s condition, his mother, Gohl, made sure Turbiak knew 'that [J.G.'s] head area was very fragile' when she enrolled him in Turbiak's classroom at Webster Elementary School."

"But the majority does not stop there. It goes on to state that no jury could find excessive force when a special education teacher grabs a severely brain injured three-year-old child by the head and violently jerks it back."

"[A] reasonable, even compelling, inference from the record is that Turbiak's abuse inhibited disabled children like J.G. from being educated appropriately."

"All that matters here is that Gohl has presented enough evidence to create a genuine issue of material fact on each of her claims, and, as a result, her case should go to a jury. For these reasons, this case should be reversed and remanded. I respectfully dissent."

COPAA filed an Amicus brief with the Court in this case.(Parent's attorney - Christopher P. Desmond // School's attorney - Gourgi G. Sashital)

Outcome: School district prevailed.[208]

[208] A Petition for Certiorari to SCOTUS is pending.

Montesa v. Schwartz + East Ramapo
2nd Cir. 2016
New York - 9/12/2016

This case was filed by several hundred New York parents against a dozen individual defendants and the East Ramapo Central School District alleging a violation of the "Establishment Clause of the First Amendment to the United States Constitution." The Establishment Clause states "Congress shall make no law respecting an establishment of religion . . ."[209]

The parents also alleged that attorney "D'Agostino devised an IDEA settlement scheme to divert public money into private religious schools . . . According to the plaintiff's Complaint, at School Board meetings D'Agostino exhibited an extremely combative and alienating style that offended and antagonized the community members who are opposed to the School Board's actions."

The District Court ruled in favor of the parents, finding that the parents had "standing" to bring the lawsuit and found that the "Board Members are not entitled to qualified immunity." Two of the three Judges of the Court of Appeals reversed the District Court and the case was dismissed. This is a complex case about issues of "standing" and whether the parents and/or their children have sustained or will sustain injury from the acts complained about and whether the Court has the power to provide a remedy.

The Court of Appeals opened this case by explaining that the parents ". . . allege that a majority of the East Ramapo School District Board ('School Board') are of the Orthodox/Hasidic Jewish faith or are sympathetic to the interests of the Orthodox/Hasidic Jewish community ('Board Defendants'). The Student-Plaintiffs claim that over the last decade the Board Defendants have siphoned money out of the public school system and into yeshivas and other religious organizations for the benefit of the Hasidic children's religious education and the Board Defendants' shared religious community. The Student-Plaintiffs allege that the Board Defendants have promoted the Hasidic Jewish faith in violation of the First Amendment to the United States Constitution by (1) systematically funding Hasidic schools with public monies by manipulating the Individuals with Disabilities Education Act ('IDEA') settlement process, (2) providing preferential treatment to Hasidic Institutions when they attempted to sell and lease two school buildings, and (3) buying religious books with public money and loaning the books to Hasidic schools."

"The Board Members argue that the students lack standing because they did not suffer a direct injury resulting from a violation of the Establishment Clause. The Board Members further contend that even if the students have standing, the Board Members are entitled to absolute and qualified immunity. We hold that the Students lack standing to pursue their Establishment Clause claims, and therefore those claims must be dismissed."

In a strongly worded dissent, Judge Reiss stated: "In characterizing Student-Plaintiffs' injuries as 'too far removed, too attenuated, from the alleged unconstitutional component of the act of funneling public monies to support the advancement of Orthodox Hasidic Jewish schools,' the majority ignores the fact that the Student-Plaintiffs' educational harm arises directly out of the allegedly unconstitutional acts, the general public, including taxpayers, are not suffering this same injury, and Student-Plaintiffs could not assert Establishment Clause claims if the District diverted the same funds for a secular purpose. As a result, Student-Plaintiffs' alleged injuries are not 'similar to that of any other individual who is affected by the District's budget, regardless of whether that person is an employee, a student, a vendor, a taxpayer, or a citizen,' and they do not allege a 'generalized grievance . . . [that would be] most appropriately addressed in the representative branches.' Moreover, no other class of plaintiffs can assert this same claim or is better situated to assert a deprivation of this same interest."

"Although the majority points out that the Student-Plaintiffs fail to cite precedent authorizing their Establishment Clause claim, it is equally true that there is no precedent prohibiting it."

(Parent's attorney - Laura D. Barbieri // Defendant's attorney - David J. Butler)

Outcome: School district prevailed.

[209] See the February 16, 2016 *Oliver v. Hofmeister* case from Oklahoma, in which religious and private schools were an issue, although the nature of the litigation was different.

BC v. Mt. Vernon Sch. Dist.
837 F.3d 152 (2nd Cir. 2016)
New York - 9/16/2016

The parents alleged violations of IDEA, ADA, and Section 504 of the Rehabilitation Act: "Plaintiffs' claims focus on the District's provision of academic intervention services to J.C. and T.H. during regular school hours. AIS courses are non-credit-bearing courses intended for students at risk of not meeting state performance standards. Plaintiffs contend that the provision of AIS courses during regular school hours - at the expense of credit-bearing courses - interfered with the ability of their children to meet the schools' credit requirements each year and violated the IDEA, ADA, and Section 504."

With regard to the AIS claims - "Mindful that NYSED regulations do not actually mandate - but instead merely permit - that AIS take place during regular school hours, Plaintiffs rely on a theory of 'deliberate indifference' on the part of the NYSED 'to the strong likelihood' of ADA and Section 504 violations resulting from the regulations. The district court properly concluded that Plaintiffs failed to allege deliberate indifference."

The District Court dismissed the ADA and Section 504 claims against the defendants. The Court of Appeals affirmed. The District Court also found that the parents failed to exhaust their administrative remedies[210] and dismissed the IDEA claims. Regarding the failure to exhaust, the Court of Appeals, in upholding the District Court noted that: "It is undisputed that Plaintiffs failed to exhaust their administrative remedies. Plaintiffs assert that exhaustion would have been futile, so as to excuse them from this requirement, because the District Defendants failed to implement the services specified in the IEP. We have stated, however, that the mere fact that a 'school has failed to implement services that were specified or otherwise clearly stated in an IEP' does not suffice to excuse a plaintiff from the exhaustion requirement."

This September 16, 2016 decision by Judge Livingston was issued as two separate Opinions, simultaneously. One Opinion is titled "Summary Order" and provides a limited overview of the legal and factual issues. The second Opinion provides J.C.'s detailed factual educational history and analysis of educational academic credits. The legal analysis focuses on the difference between a "child with a disability" as defined by IDEA and a "qualified individual with a disability" as defined by ADA and Section 504. Both Opinions are merged in this summary of *B.C. v. Mt. Vernon.*

"Plaintiffs do not rely upon and have not placed into the record any particularized evidence to show that individual students included in their data who are classified as having a 'disability' pursuant to the IDEA also satisfy the ADA and Section 504 'disability' definitions."

In other words, being an IDEA child with a disability does not automatically mean that the child is qualified under the ADA and Section 504. In this instance, the focus was not on J.C., the individual child, but instead on the class of children with IEPs who needed AIS services, in an attempt to prove a systemic violation of ADA and 504 pursuant to those AIS procedures. Plaintiffs were attempting to use statistical evidence to show a disparate impact created by the procedures.

"For these reasons, an IDEA disability is not equivalent to a disability as cognizable under ADA and Section 504. Plaintiffs, therefore, cannot rely solely on 'receipt of special education' to establish an ADA or Section 504 disability. Those seeking relief pursuant to ADA or Section 504 must come forward with 'additional evidence' - beyond simply their eligibility for IDEA coverage - showing their eligibility for the remedies afforded by the ADA and Section 504."

"The Court of Appeals upheld the dismissal against the parents."

(Parent's attorney - Michael H. Sussman // School's attorney - Lewis R. Silverman)

Outcome: School district and NY SDE prevailed.

[210] See SCOTUS decision in *Fry*.

Pollack v. Regional Sch. Unit 75
1st Cir. 2016
Maine - 10/4/2016

In this case about accommodations, SCOTUS *Fry* exhaustion, and procedures, the primary issue was the child's use of an audio recording device.

BP is a "seventeen-year-old student at Regional School Unit 75 (the 'District') who is diagnosed with autism, cognitive impairment, and a variant of Landau-Kleffner Syndrome, which affects his ability to understand and express language. B.P. is nonverbal and therefore cannot communicate with his parents about his school day the way a student without his disabilities can."

As the result of an incident at school, the parents sought the school's consent to permit their child to wear an audio recording device to school. The district denied the request and litigation followed. The subsequent legal history and proceedings became quite convoluted.

The parent's due process "complaint alleged that, by refusing to allow B.P. to wear a recording device, the District had failed to make a reasonable accommodation under Title II of the Americans with Disabilities Act, and thereby impaired the Parents' ability to obtain information about B.P.'s school day and his education." After a three-day hearing, the hearing officer denied the parents request.

The parents appealed and "the district court granted summary judgment for the District on the ADA, Section 504, and First Amendment claims relating to the recording device prohibition, on the grounds that the Parents failed to exhaust the IDEA administrative process . . ."

However, shortly before the Court's dismissal order, the Parents filed a new due process complaint, this time alleging that the refusal "deprived B.P. of a free appropriate public education as required by the IDEA." Another Special Education Due Process Hearing occurred and, on June 2, 2016, that claim was denied by a hearing officer."

"[B]oth parties agreed that the Parents have satisfied the exhaustion requirement as articulated by the district court . . ."

"[T]he Parents still seek a determination on the merits of their ADA, Section 504, and First Amendment claims. The District urges us to dismiss the appeal and leave the judgment below intact. The Parents, on the other hand, argue that we should . . . remand to the district court for consideration on the merits."

The Parents "took the actions necessary to clear the procedural hurdle of exhaustion in accordance with the district court's order. The Parents have already undergone lengthy litigation in both administrative and federal forums to achieve resolution of their claims; the only bar remaining to a determination of the merits of these claims was this issue of exhaustion. Now that they have undoubtedly exhausted the process required by the IDEA, it would be inequitable to leave the summary judgment order standing and have these claims dismissed without ever reaching their merits."

"Accordingly, we dismiss the appeal as moot, vacate the portion of the district court's order granting summary judgment for the District on the ADA, Section 504, and First Amendment claims relating to B.P.'s right to wear a recording device at school, and remand for determination of the merits of those claims. Vacated and Remanded."

(Parent's attorney - Richard L. O'Meara // School's attorney - Nathaniel A. Bessey)

Outcome: Parents prevailed.

Dervishi v. Stamford Bd. of Ed.. and CTDOE
2nd Cir. 2016
Connecticut - 10/6/2016

The parent filed a 'pro se'[211] Complaint in federal court against the school district and the state department of education, without having first sought a special education due process hearing. This SCOTUS *Fry* 'failure to exhaust' administrative remedies' was fatal.

The district court dismissed the case and the parent appealed to the Second Circuit.

[211] Parent did not retain an attorney, represented herself.

"Plaintiff-appellant Shkelqesa Dervishi, proceeding pro se, appeals from the district court's judgment dismissing, for lack of subject matter jurisdiction, her complaint alleging that defendant-appellee Stamford Board of Education (the 'Board') denied her son a free appropriate public education ('FAPE') for the 2011-12, 2012-13, 2013-14, and 2014-15 school years in violation of the Individuals with Disabilities Education Act ('IDEA'). She also asserted claims under the Americans with Disabilities Act ('ADA'), the Rehabilitation Act ('Rehab Act'), and 42 U.S.C. § 1983."

"The IDEA requires an aggrieved party to exhaust all administrative remedies before bringing an action in federal court. A district court lacks subject matter jurisdiction if a plaintiff fails to exhaust her administrative remedies when 'assert[ing] claims for relief available under the IDEA, regardless of the statutory basis of [her] complaint.'

However, exhaustion is excused if the defendant failed to notify the plaintiff of her procedural rights under the IDEA. Exhaustion is also excused under the 'futility exception' if a plaintiff can show that administrative review would not have provided an adequate remedy. The party seeking to invoke the exception bears the burden of showing futility."

"Dervishi does not contend in her brief that she exhausted her administrative remedies. Instead, she argues that the district court should have excused her failure to exhaust because the Board did not notify her of her procedural rights under the IDEA and an administrative proceeding would have been inadequate because any hearing officer would have been biased. Dervishi also argues that exhaustion was not required for her damages claims.

Her arguments are without merit. First, as the district court reasoned, the record shows that the Board gave Dervishi sufficient notice of her procedural rights under the IDEA. Second, the record does not suggest that administrative review would have been unfair or biased and Dervishi presents no compelling arguments suggesting otherwise. Finally, the IDEA exhaustion requirement applies to claims seeking monetary damages. For these reasons, we conclude that the district court did not err in dismissing Dervishi's claims."

"We have considered Dervishi's remaining arguments and find them to be without merit. Accordingly, we AFFIRM the judgment of the district court."

(Parent's attorney - none, *pro se* // School's attorney - Patrick M. Fahey)

Outcome: School district prevailed.

NG v. ABC Unif. Sch. Dist.

9th Cir. 2016

California - 11/3/2016

During the Chino Valley student's hospitalization, she received special education services from the ABC Unified School District where the hospital was located. Post discharge planning recommended a residential placement and the parent requested that the ABC School District pay for that placement. They refused. Parent appealed, lost at Due Process and at the District Court. On appeal to the Ninth Circuit, they explained that "California Education Code provides that the District's responsibility over a hospitalized student is the period when the student is 'placed in a public hospital . . . for medical purposes. . . [T]he District does not have the responsibility to provide post-discharge education to the student." Under California Government Code, the responsibility for post-discharge educational placement is on the 'receiving local educational agency'. . . Hence, the ABC Unified School District was not responsible for N.G.'s post-charge RTC placement." The District Court's ruling was affirmed.

Outcome: School district prevailed.

Cobb County Sch. Dist. v. DB.

11th Cir. 2016

Per Curiam

Georgia - 11/14/2016

This **2016 Case of the Year** involves a reverse due process hearing filed by a Georgia school district that cost them substantial attorneys' fees paid to parent's counsel. "[T]he posture of the parties in this case is different from the typical IDEA action. Here, the District brought an administrative action in response to a request from Defendants for an independent educational evaluation ('IEE')'. Defendants claim that the District's evaluation was inappropriate and inadequate for planning D.B.'s IEP and, accordingly, violated rights established under 20 U.S.C. § 1415(b)."

"An administrative hearing was held in the Georgia Office of State Administrative Hearings over seven days . . . On June 3, 2014, the

Administrative Law Judge ('ALJ') issued a final decision ('Final Decision,') . . . [finding] that 'Cooper's FBA is not appropriate because the data collection, as designed, was never going to provide a reliable enough conclusion as to the functions of D.B.'s serious and problematic behaviors.'"

"Based upon her findings, the ALJ granted Defendants' request for an IEE at public expense. Plaintiff appealed to this [U.S. District] Court."[212]

After prevailing in U. S. District Court, the parents filed a petition for attorney's fees in the amount of $271,527.50. The Court awarded $75,000.00 and parents appealed the attorney fee ruling to the Eleventh Circuit.

On appeal, the Court explained: "On appeal, the defendants argue that the district court erred, inter alia, by improperly reducing their attorneys' fees award based on factors listed in § 1415(i)(3)(F) of the Act."

"We review the district court's award of attorneys' fees and costs for abuse of discretion, revisiting questions of law de novo."

"Without calculations or citations to authority, it is difficult to meaningfully review how the district court interpreted and applied the provisions of § 1415(i)(3). ('A court's order on attorney's fees must allow meaningful appellate review. The trial court should articulate and give principled reasons for its decisions and show some calculations. If the court disallows hours, it must explain which hours are disallowed and show why an award of those hours would be improper.'). However, we hold the district court abused its discretion to the extent that it reduced the Appellants' fee award under § 1415(i)(3)(F). Under the plain language of the statute, the district court cannot reduce a prevailing party's fee award pursuant to § 1415(i)(3)(F) when 'the court finds that the State or local educational agency unreasonably protracted the final resolution of the action or proceeding.' 20 U.S.C. § 1415(i)(3)(G). Here, the district court made findings that both parties had 'needlessly extended' and 'over-litigated the case.'"

"Therefore, we vacate the district court's award of attorneys' fees and costs, and we remand for the court to recalculate the award of 'reasonable attorneys' fees.'"

(Parents' attorney - Jonathan Zimring[213] // School's attorney - Patrick H. Ouzts)

Outcome: Parents prevailed.[214]

NE v. Seattle Sch. Dist.

842 F.3d 1093 (9th Cir. 2016)

Washington - 11/17/2016

In this is a "stay-put" or "pendency" case,[215] the Bellevue School District proposed a two part IEP. For the duration of the school year, the child would remain in the present educational setting and, at the beginning of the next academic year, would be placed into a self-contained special education class.

The parents agreed to their son remaining in the present placement for the duration of the school year, but objected to the proposed change of placement for the next academic year. They did not seek a special education due process hearing at that time. Instead, the parents moved from Bellevue to Seattle.

"The [Seattle] school district, however, reviewed N.E.'s records and proposed placing him in a self-contained class similar to the one embodied in stage two of the [Bellevue] May 2015 IEP. Plaintiffs objected on September 9, 2015, and filed an administrative due process challenge. Plaintiffs also filed a 'stay-put' motion, pursuant to 20 U.S.C. §1415(j), arguing that N.E.'s stay-put placement was the general education class described in the December 2014 IEP. Defendant resisted the stay-put motion and argued that the self-contained class described in the May 2015 IEP was N.E.'s stay-put placement."

"An administrative law judge agreed with Defendant and determined that the self-contained class was N.E.'s stay-put placement. Plaintiffs appealed that decision and filed a motion with the district court seeking a temporary restraining order

---

[212] **Wrightslaw note**: the preceding paragraphs were taken directly from the District Court's September 28, 2015 Decision in favor of the parents.

[213] This is the same Zimring in *Olmstead v. L.C. ex rel. Zimring*, 527 U.S. 581 (1999)

[214] **Update:** After this case was remanded, the District Court entered an Order on January 17, 2017 finding Cobb County "needlessly extended the litigation. . . Therefore, Defendants are awarded $271,527.50 as attorneys' fees related to the original action. As prevailing parties, they are also entitled to fees associated with the appeal."

[215] **Wrightslaw note**: Because of different definitions used by different Courts of Appeal, this statute is known as either the "Stay-Put" statute or the "Pendency" statute.

and a preliminary injunction. . . The district court denied Plaintiffs' motion . . . Plaintiffs timely appeal."

"The pivotal issue is what 'educational placement' was 'then-current,' 20 U.S.C. § 1415(j), after N.E.'s family moved to Seattle in the summer of 2015 but before the 2015-16 school year began. Plaintiffs contend that the 'then current educational placement' must be the educational setting in which N.E. was enrolled either before his May 2015 IEP or, in the alternative, during the first stage of the May 2015 IEP. Defendant counters that the 'then-current educational placement' for the 2015-16 school year is the setting described in the second stage of the May 2015 IEP. We agree with Defendant and, accordingly, affirm the district court's denial of injunctive relief."

"The IDEA does not define 'then-current educational placement.' The reading most consistent with the ordinary meaning of the phrase suggests that the 'then-current educational placement' refers to the educational setting in which the student is actually enrolled at the time the parents request a due process hearing to challenge a proposed change in the child's educational placement.'"

"But two conceptual difficulties complicate the analysis. First, during the hiatus between school years, it is artificial to refer to remaining in a then-current placement; literally, there is none. Second, when an IEP contains two stages, determining the 'then-current educational placement' requires one to look either backward or forward."

"In short, the December 2014 IEP was superseded. The May 2015 IEP encompassed both the individual class and the self-contained class stages. Plaintiffs did not challenge the May 2015 IEP despite having had months to do so before the scheduled implementation of its second phase in September 2015. The May 2015 IEP had already been implemented (and the scheduled start date for stage two had already passed) by the time Plaintiffs requested a due process hearing and, thus, was N.E.'s 'then-current educational placement.'"

By a vote of two to one, the Court of Appeals affirmed the decision of the District Court. Circuit Court Judge Berzon filed a strong dissent, below.

"The majority applies the IDEA's 'stay-put' provision to allow N.E. to be placed in an entirely new learning environment, more restrictive than any in which he had previously been enrolled, over his parents' objection. The 'stay-put' provision was designed precisely to preclude transferring students to new, more restrictive environments while their parents challenge the transfer."

"The 'stay-put' provision, as I have explained, focuses not on what is contained in the IEP document but on the child's actual educational experience."

"Here, N.E. had never experienced the self-contained classroom program the 2015 IEP proposed. A child cannot 'stay-put' in a program in which he never took part; the 'then-current educational placement' cannot be an educational setting the child has never experienced. From the child's point of view, moving him to an entirely new kind of educational experience, one that exists only on paper, is precisely the sort of fundamental disruption the 'stay-put' provision was designed to prevent."

'The preservation of the status quo [is meant to] ensure that the student remains in the last placement that the parents and the educational authority agreed to be appropriate.'"

(Parent's attorney - Lara Hruska and David T. Hokit // School's attorney - Lauren Rebecca Hruska)

Outcome: School district prevailed.

Campbell v. Lamar Inst. of Tech.
5th Cir. 2016
Texas - 11/23/2016

This higher education[216] 504 / ADA case is about denial of a disability accommodations.

"Because LIT's denial of Campbell's accommodation request was reasonable, we AFFIRM the district court's grant of summary judgment in favor of LIT."

"Russell Campbell is a former student at Lamar Institute of Technology (LIT) where he earned an Associate's Degree in Emergency Medical Services (EMS) and subsequently enrolled in LIT's Respiratory Care Program. Due to an anoxic brain injury, Campbell struggles to retain and process information. While he was enrolled in the EMS program, LIT accommodated his learning disability by extending time for all of his exams and providing

[216] IDEA is not applicable in higher educational disputes, only 504 / ADA.

a laptop and a recorder to help with note-taking during class."

"In response to his declining performance, . . . Campbell requested that, . . . he be permitted to take two exams in each class: one at the same time as the other students and another two weeks later. Alternatively, he requested two extra weeks of study time after the other students had taken the exam (which would also require creation of a second exam to prevent cheating)."

". . . Cole and Jefferson determined that Campbell's requested additional accommodation would be unreasonable because it would give Campbell an unfair advantage over his classmates and would burden professors by requiring them to modify their teaching or testing schedules."

[The other professors later] "informed him that they would only provide him with the originally approved accommodations and would not alter the testing schedule. . . Campbell withdrew from LIT later that day."

"Shortly thereafter, Campbell filed a grievance to the Dean of Instruction based upon the denial of his requested accommodations . . . Less than a month later, Reynard responded to the grievance and stated that LIT would provide reasonable accommodations supported by medical documentation and would waive tuition and fees for the next semester. Campbell rejected this offer. In his deposition, Campbell stated that he would not return to LIT because he does not feel wanted."

"Nine months later . . . Campbell sued LIT, as well as Cole, Jefferson, Walden, and Reynard (collectively, 'defendants') in their official capacities, seeking compensatory damages and declaratory and injunctive relief."

"Because LIT's denial of Campbell's accommodation request was reasonable, we AFFIRM the district court's grant of summary judgment in favor of LIT."

Even though the Court upheld the District Court's dismissal, the Court clarified immunity. "The district court erred in concluding that LIT is entitled to sovereign immunity. Eleventh Amendment sovereign immunity does not bar Campbell's Rehabilitation Act claim for money damages. State entities that accept federal funding knowingly and voluntarily waive their sovereign immunity to suit under § 504 of the Rehabilitation Act."

"Campbell asserts discrimination under the Rehabilitation Act. The ADA's language generally tracks the language of the Rehabilitation Act and expressly states that the 'remedies, procedures and rights' of the Rehabilitation Act are obtainable under the ADA. 42 U.S.C. § 12133'" citing *Delano-Pyle.*[217]

Attorney for student - Laurence Wade Watts // Attorney for Institute - Susan Marie Watson

Outcome: Lamar Institute of Technology prevailed.

Powers v. Northside Indep. Sch. Dist.
5th Cir. 2016
Texas - 12/5/2016

Two school administrators blew the whistle on their school district "to report NISD's purportedly unlawful conduct in denying disabled students accommodations to which they were entitled." They were terminated because they found students eligible for Section 504 accommodations. They appealed the termination and alleged a violation of the Whistleblower Act.[218] The school district asserted immunity. The District Court would not grant immunity and the School District appealed to the Fifth Circuit.

"Plaintiffs-appellees Don Powers and Karon Wernli are a former principal and assistant principal, respectively, at Adams Hill Elementary School in San Antonio, Texas, located within

---

[217] *Delano-Pyle v. Victoria City* 302 F.3d 567, 574 (5th Cir. 2002). As such, the "[j]urisprudence interpreting either section is applicable to both . . ."

[218] **Wrightslaw note:** For another whistleblower / Qui Tam case filed by a school employee, see the Watertown NY case. The school's speech therapist alleged that her school district improperly billed the federal government for Medicaid reimbursement. The federal government recovered Five Hundred and Forty Million Dollars and she was awarded Ten Million Dollars. For more, google: whistleblower watertown medicaid.

Northside Independent School District (NISD), the defendant-appellant in this case. NISD terminated their employment after determining that they had improperly implemented the federal Rehabilitation Act. In response, Powers and Wernli sued NISD under, among other things, the Texas Whistleblower Act, claiming their termination constituted unlawful retaliation for their reports of NISD's alleged violations of the Rehabilitation Act. NISD moved for summary judgment, raising governmental immunity as a defense to the Whistleblower Act claims. The district court denied NISD's motion in relevant part, and NISD now appeals."

"To comply with the section 504 requirements, NISD created a '504 committee' comprising educators tasked with conducting the required evaluations of students. Powers and Wernli were members of the 504 committee during the 2012-2013 school year. That year, the Section 504 committee evaluated J.B., a student with attention deficit hyperactivity disorder. The Section 504 committee determined that J.B. had a reading disability and was thus entitled to an accommodation during the 2013 STAAR test, which is a Texas standardized test. Pursuant to the accommodation, a proctor would read the test questions aloud to J.B. Shortly thereafter, NISD's 504 coordinator, Anna Draker, reviewed the 504 committee's recommendation and notified the 504 committee that J.B. was not entitled to the accommodation due to a lack of supporting documentation. As a result, J.B. did not receive the accommodation."

"After Draker's intervention in the J.B. matter, she audited NISD's 504 files during which she discovered that Wernli had marked as eligible various students who Draker believed were ineligible for section 504 accommodations. Draker and other NISD personnel then informed Powers and Wernli that they believed these practices were illegal. After those conversations, Powers and Wernli made several calls to the Texas Education Agency (TEA). They testified in their depositions that they made these calls to report NISD's purportedly unlawful conduct in denying disabled students accommodations to which they were entitled."

". . . NISD suspended Powers and Wernli on the ground that they had illegally classified students as eligible for section 504 accommodations . . . [later] the NISD Board of Trustees voted to terminate Powers's and Wernli's employment . . ."

After the termination, "Powers and Wernli filed this suit, alleging in part that NISD terminated their employment in violation of the Texas Whistleblower Act."

NISD asserted that they had immunity, which was rejected by the District Court. NISD appealed the denial of immunity to the Fifth Circuit, which explained that "When a public employee alleges a violation of the Act, the employing state or local governmental entity's immunity from suit is waived."

The case was remanded back to the District Court. An "Alternative Dispute Resolution" (ADR) settlement conference was held on February 28, 2017 and counsel advised the Court that they were unable to resolve the case. The District Court has created a "Scheduling Order" with discovery to be completed by May, 2018 and possible Jury Trial date in October, 2018.

(Plaintiff's attorney - Mark W. Robinett // School's attorney - Maureen Scott Franco)

Outcome: The two terminated employees prevailed.[219]

Forest Grove Sch. Dist. v. Student
9th Cir. 2016
Oregon - 12/5/2016

The Court of Appeals provided very few facts in this case, explaining that "Student appeals the district court's order reversing in part a decision by the administrative law judge ('ALJ') . . ."

"The excerpts of record in this case are sealed, so our disposition does not repeat the facts, which are known to the parties."[220]

---

[219] **Update:** The case was remanded back to the District Court. An "Alternative Dispute Resolution" (ADR) settlement conference was held on February 28, 2017 and counsel advised the Court that they were unable to resolve the case. The District Court created a "Scheduling Order" with discovery to be completed by May, 2018 and possible Jury Trial date in October, 2018.

[220] The facts can be found in the District Court decision issued by Judge Acosta in Civ. No. 3:12-cv-01837-AC.

The District Court Judge explained that the Administrative Law Judge ruled in the parent and child's favor on almost all issues, including a denial to the parents of the "opportunity to meaningfully participate in the Student's education during the 2009-2010, 2010-2011, and 2011-2012 academic years . . . failed to identify Student as a student with a disability in all areas of disability during the 2009-2010, 2010-2011 and 2011-2012 academic years, . . . failed to evaluate Student in all areas of suspected disability . . . failed to provide Student with a free appropriate public education (FAPE) . . ."

"The ALJ ordered the District to provide . . . a comprehensive evaluation . . . a new IEP . . . direct transitional reading instruction . . . transition math instruction . . . anxiety counseling . . . driver's education . . . training for District staff on IDEA protocol for writing and implementing IEPs."

The District appealed the ALJ's decision to the U.S. District Court alleging errors the factual and legal analysis and requested that the ALJ's decision be reversed.

The District Court was unimpressed with the ALJ's Due Process Decision. "Although the ALJ's sixty-eight-page single spaced opinion is lengthy, it is not careful and thorough, and the court affords it little deference. The ALJ describes in detail many of the exhibits on record. She includes large block quotes of each IEP, and describes each IEP meeting as described in the IEP meeting notes. However, the ALJ makes little to no mention of witness testimony taken over multiple days of administrative hearing. Most importantly, the ALJ does not discuss the hearing testimony of the parties' experts, which sheds significant light on the issues presently before the court and often contradict the ALJ's conclusions of fact and law."

"The ALJ's conclusions of law are also entitled to little deference. In her analysis of the issues, the ALJ fails to adequately support her conclusions with caselaw."

"Because the ALJ's opinion is factually selective to the detriment of an accurate factual record and inadequately develops the applicable legal standards, the court affords the ALJ's opinion little deference."

"The court vacates all but one aspect of the ALJ's remedies award. First, the court determined that the District met all of its duties to evaluate Student for suspected disabilities, . . . requiring the District to provide a driver's education course is inappropriate. . . ordering the District to educate Student in all classes using the 'Larsen method' exceeded the ALJ's authority . . . the ALJ's award of compensatory instruction in those subjects is inappropriate. Fifth, although the District committed several IDEA violations, they were not so numerous or so extreme as to require all District personnel to undergo training on proper IDEA procedure."

On appeal, the Ninth Circuit explained that "We agree with the district court that the ALJ's opinion is entitled to little deference . . ."

"To show harm, procedural inadequacies generally must result in the loss of an educational opportunity or seriously infringe the parents' opportunity to participate in the formulation of a student's individualized education plan. Even assuming that the School District did not comply strictly with IDEA procedures, Student has not shown that the failure[s] . . . affected her or her parents' substantive rights."

"Likewise, the School District did not violate Student's substantive rights . . . an 'appropriate' public education need not be the 'absolutely best;' it must only provide 'a basic floor of opportunity' that is 'individually designed to provide individual benefit.' . . . Student has not shown that the School District failed to provide her with a free appropriate public education."

The ruling of the District Court was affirmed by the Court of Appeals.

(Parent's attorney - Diane F. Wiscarson // School's attorney - Richard G. Cohn-Lee)

Outcome: School prevailed.[221]

They span numerous IEPs over the years with multiple factual and legal issues.

[221] **Update:** We have been advised that a portion of the case is before the District Court to determine "transition services still owed."

Emma C v. Eastin + CA DOE
9th Cir. 2016
California - 12/8/2016

This case began more than 20 years ago and relates to the power of a Court Appointed Monitor to force compliance.

This is case # 3:96-cv-04179 presided by Judge Thelton E. Henderson of the U. S. District Court for the Northern District of California. It involves a Consent Decree, has numerous plaintiffs and a long history. The District Court's docket sheet, has more than 2,000 entries.

The Court of Appeals noted that the California Department of Education, State Board of Education and Superintendent of Public Instruction, "(collectively 'the State')" "appeal the district court's orders requiring the parties to develop and implement a corrective action plan ('Action Plan'). . . [which was] designed to ensure that the [State's] monitoring system would be adequate to guarantee that the Ravenswood City School District ('Ravenswood') continues to satisfy its obligations under the parties' first amended consent decree ('Consent Decree') . . ."

"The parties entered into the Consent Decree to bring Ravenswood and the State into compliance with the Individuals with Disabilities Education Act ('IDEA')."

While not included in this Court of Appeals decision, from a review of the Court's file and January 16, 2017 correspondence to the parties from Court Monitor Mark Mlawer, and subsequent January 20, 2017 ruling from the District Court, the underlying issue was that the "Defendant California Department of Education ('CDE') recently decided to ignore the procedure it agreed to over eleven years ago to provide the Monitor with information he needs to evaluate whether CDE is complying with the First Amended Consent Decree ('FACD') in this case. This is simply unacceptable. The [District] Court issues this order to confirm – lest there was any doubt – that CDE must provide the Monitor with information necessary to fulfill his duties, and that failure to do so will be punishable by contempt."

"CDE cannot decide unilaterally to violate long-standing procedures developed by the Monitor in consultation with the parties, or to ignore requests for information from the Monitor pursuant to his obligations. The Court issues this order to make clear that CDE must, and shall, respond promptly to all requests for information from the Monitor concerning CDE's performance of its obligations to ensure the provision of FAPE in the LRE to children with disabilities in Ravenswood."

"The [District] Court intends this order to provide a basis for entering sanctions should CDE fail to provide the Monitor with the information discussed above. Sanctions may include contempt proceedings against the responsible person or persons identified by CDE."[222]

It appears that the California Department of Education attempted to unilaterally change the terms of the consent decree with the District Court, was unsuccessful, appealed to the Ninth Circuit and again, was unsuccessful. The threat of sanctions and contempt of court remains alive.

The Court of Appeals noted that the California Department of Education, State Board of Education and Superintendent of Public Instruction, "(collectively 'the State')" "appeal the district court's orders requiring the parties to develop and implement a corrective action plan ('Action Plan'). . . [which was] designed to ensure that the [State's] monitoring system would be adequate to guarantee that the Ravenswood City School District ('Ravenswood') continues to satisfy its obligations under the parties' first amended consent decree ('Consent Decree') . . ."

"The parties entered into the Consent Decree to bring Ravenswood and the State into compliance with the Individuals with Disabilities Education Act ('IDEA')."

"In addition, we note that the State has waited more than a decade to raise its argument that the plaintiffs have no private right of action . . . By waiting so long and signing the Consent Decree, the State has waived this defense." "We affirm."

(Parent's attorney - Arlene Brynne Mayerson // CA DOE attorney - Darrell Warren Spence)

Outcome: Parents and Court Appointed Monitor prevailed.

---

[222] **Wrightslaw note**: Source for the preceding three paragraphs: U. S. District Court Order January 20, 2017.

Reed v. DCPS
843 F.3d 517 (DC Cir. 2016)
DC - 12/9/2016

Parent's attorneys sought their fees in this Washington, DC case. While the District Court awarded attorneys' fees, it was not the full amount desired. This appeal followed.

"Appellants contend that the District Court erred in excluding certain hours spent at 'settlement conferences' from their fee award. Appellants also assert that the District Court abused its discretion in refusing to find that the 'prevailing market rate' for attorneys' fees in IDEA cases is aligned with the *Laffey* Matrix, a fee matrix originally compiled to reflect the prevailing market rate for 'complex federal litigation.'

"We agree with Appellants that the District Court should not have excluded certain hours billed as 'settlement conferences' from its initial fee award calculation. However, we hold that the District Court did not abuse its discretion in finding that Appellants had failed to demonstrate that their IDEA matters fall within the category of 'complex federal litigation' to which the *Laffey* Matrix applies. Therefore, the District Court was not obliged to follow the *Laffey* Matrix in calculating attorneys' fees due Appellants."

With regard to the 'settlement conference' issue, the Court noted that "Appellants are correct that the District Court abused its discretion in excluding certain hours classified as 'settlement conferences' in their billing records from their fee award. IDEA makes clear that hours spent in 'resolution sessions' are non-reimbursable and, thus, should not be included in a prevailing party's fee award. However, the statute delineates a number of requirements for a meeting to constitute a 'resolution session': it must be attended by the parents who have submitted a complaint, 'the relevant member or members of the [Individualized Education Program ('IEP')] Team who have specific knowledge of the facts identified in the complaint,' and a 'representative of the [local educational] agency who has decision making authority on behalf of such agency.'"

The Court agreed with parent's counsel that the purported Resolution Sessions were 'sham resolution sessions,' which fell short of the standards prescribed by IDEA and thus, as settlement conferences, an award of attorneys' fees was proper and reversed the District Court.

While the Court of Appeals declined, in this instance, to apply the "*Laffey* Matrix," Judge Tatel's Concurring Opinion opened the door to its application in the future.

"IDEA and Title VII litigation share many other complexities. Both involve sophisticated non-legal subjects: in Title VII litigation, statistics, employment testing, and workplace compensation; in IDEA litigation, child psychology, speech and language pathology, occupational therapy, physical therapy, and special education curricula. Both types of litigation rely heavily on experts in a variety of fields: in Title VII, statisticians and psychologists; in IDEA, childhood development specialists, psychiatrists, pathologists, and experts in educational options for children with disabilities. Finally, both types of litigation often involve complex organizations: large companies in Title VII cases; large public school systems (here DCPS) in IDEA cases."

"For these reasons, were this panel not bound by *Eley*, I would hold, as a matter of law, that IDEA litigation is sufficiently complex to warrant *Laffey* rates.

(Parent's attorney - Douglas Tyrka // School's attorney -Richard S. Love)

Outcome: Parents attorney was successful is recovering attorneys' fees for the settlement conference, but the *Laffey* Matrix was not applied in this instance.

END of U.S. Court of Appeals Decisions in 2016

Chapter 4

Legal Research: How to Use Google Scholar to Find Cases

In Chapter 1, you learned that when you are researching a legal issue, you need to study the United States Code, the Federal and State Regulations, the *Commentary*, and judicial decisions, i.e., case law on your issue.

If you know a case was appealed, you need to read the earlier decisions that were appealed and reversed, or appealed and affirmed. When you read earlier decisions, you will have a clearer sense about how the law on your issue is evolving.

Chapter 3 contains a Table of Decisions in Special Education Cases by Courts of Appeals in 2016 (begins on page 44) and another Table of Decisions in Alphabetical Order (page 53). After the Table of Decisions are summaries of each decision.

Chapter 1, you learned that when you are researching a legal issue, you need to study the United States Code, the Federal and State Regulations, the Commentary, and judicial decisions, i.e., case law on your issue.

If you know a case was appealed, you need to read the earlier decisions that were appealed and reversed, or appealed and affirmed. When you read earlier decisions, you will have a clearer sense about how the law on your issue is evolving.

Chapter 3 contains a Table of Decisions in IDEA Cases by Courts of Appeals in 2016. Following the Table of Decisions are summaries of each decision. The Table of Decisions includes links to the summaries.

Tutorial: Using Google Scholar

Google Scholar allows you to search published opinions of state appellate and supreme courts since 1950, opinions from federal district, appellate, tax and bankruptcy courts since 1923, and decisions from the U.S. Supreme Court since 1791.[223]

Google Scholar embeds clickable citation links within cases. The "How Cited" tab provides the citation for that decision.

Another portion of Google Scholar searches peer-reviewed papers, theses, books, preprints, abstracts and technical reports from academic publishers, professional societies, preprint repositories and universities, and scholarly articles available on the Internet.

---

[223] https://en.wikipedia.org/wiki/Google_Scholar. Retrieved on April 1, 2017

When you use http://scholar.google.com, you can find any decision listed in the Table of Decisions. Let's find the second case listed in the Table of Decisions – *Norristown v. FC.*

Go to: http://scholar.google.com/

Click on "Case law" then "Select courts."

When the Courts page opens, go to the right column, "Federal courts," select the "Court of Appeals" for your desired Circuit (3rd Circuit) and click "Done" at the bottom of the page.

A screen will open that instructs you to "Please enter a query in the search box above." You will insert, exactly, the following, word for word, with the quotation marks -

"individuals with disabilities education act"

You will add the year (2016 in this case) or actual date of the decision and an identifiable part of the case name, "norristown." Your search query should read:

"individuals with disabilities education act" 2016 norristown

Google "legal scholar" will do a full text search of all cases in their database from the Third Circuit that have the above words in your query. You see that the decision in *Norristown School District v. F.C.* was issued on January 8, 2016.

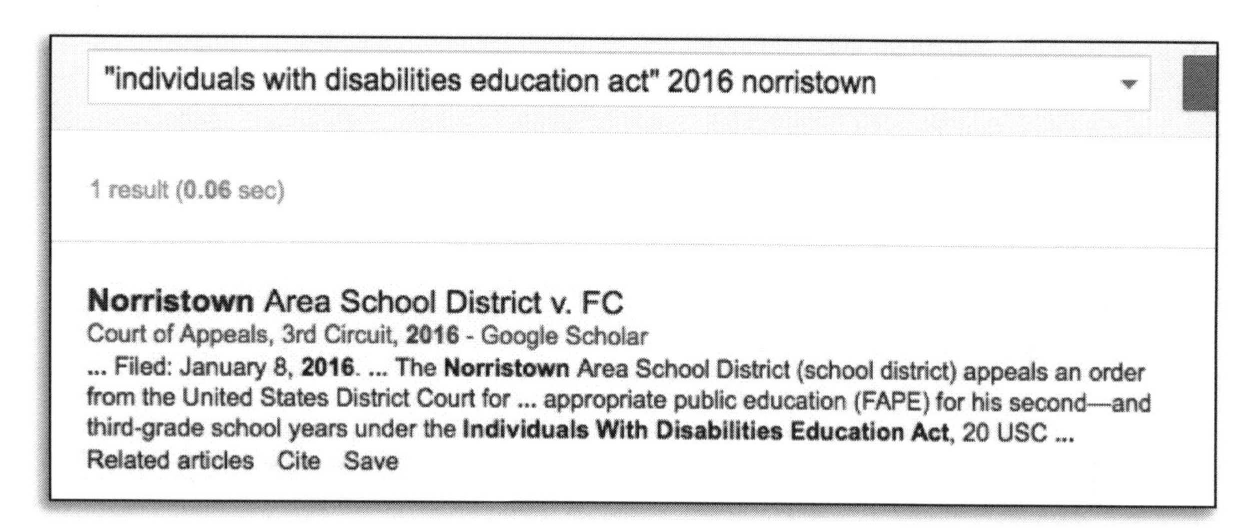

As noted earlier, most cases in the Table of Decisions do not have an "F.3d" citation. When you look up a case, be sure to click the "How Cited" tab to see if the case received a F.3d citation. Google Scholar will usually list the case and just below it, will list the case again with the F.3d citation.

You can change your search query to look for cases that have other terms — dyslexia, autism, Section 504, restraint, damages, retaliation, "individualized educational program," "IEP," "independent educational evaluation," "IEE," "Americans with Disabilities Act," etc.

When you change the courts, you can broaden your search to find cases around the country. You can even search against the name of an individual, an administrator, an expert witness, a Judge, or a school district.

Troubleshooting

On occasion, you may search for a known case and not be able to find it. When the authors were creating the database of Court of Appeals cases for our earlier book ***Wrightslaw: Special Education Legal Developments and Cases 2015***, we knew about decisions that did not appear when we searched the term "Individuals with Disabilities Education Act 2015." We were perplexed, we knew of several cases, but could not find them.

When we experimented with search terms, we found those cases. In one instance, the decision had a line break inside the word "Education." The word printed as "Educa-tion" so the Google Scholar search engine did not find it.

Two decisions from the Ninth Circuit referenced IDEA as the "Individuals with Disabilities Education Improvement Act." When we changed our search term to "Individuals with Disabilities Education Improvement Act," we found those two decisions which did not show up in our original search.

Just before press time, I conducted an experiment. I used the term "individuals with disabilities education act" 2016 to search all Courts of Appeals. Google Scholar found 121 cases. I repeated the same search but eliminated the quotation marks. The search was for cases that contained those words, without regard for the order of the words. Google Scholar found 1,610 cases.

Create a Google Scholar Alert

Go back to your original search page.

At the bottom of the page, you will see a link to "Create alert." When you create an alert, Google Scholar will send you an email alert whenever a decision is issued in the legal jurisdiction you select.

Return to the "Select courts" page. Select the Courts of Appeals for all Circuits, all U.S. District Courts in your State, and all your state courts. Change your search query to "Individuals with Disabilities Education Act" 2016.

Google will notify you of all new IDEA decisions from your federal and state courts and from all Courts of Appeal around the country in 2016.

In this chapter, you learned how to use Google Scholar to search for legal decisions. You learned how to expand and narrow your search and how to create a Google Alert.

In Summation

In the Introduction to ***Wrightslaw Special Education Legal Developments and Cases 2016***, we said this book is unique. You have special education news, trends and developments in special education law, cases from the Courts of Appeals, and our thoughts about how the law is evolving.

We may publish similar books about legal news, developments and cases annually. We appreciate your thoughts about how we can make these books better. If you wish to share your thoughts by email, please contact us at annual@wrightslaw.com.

Thank you!

Pete and Pam Wright

Index

E

F

G

H

I